Jessica Balfour

92

THE ENGLISHWOMAN'S GARDEN

*What was Paradise? but a garden, full of pleasure,
and nothing there but delights.*

WILLIAM LAWSON, 1617

THE
ENGLISHWOMAN'S
GARDEN

Edited by
Alvilde Lees-Milne
and
Rosemary Verey

CHATTO & WINDUS · LONDON · 1981

Published by
Chatto & Windus Ltd
40 William IV Street
London, WC2N 4DF

*

Clarke, Irwin & Co Ltd.
Toronto

First published March 1980
Second impression May 1980
Third impression August 1981

British Library Cataloguing in Publication Data

The Englishwoman's garden.
　　1. Flower gardening – England　　2. Women
gardeners – England
I. Lees-Milne, Alvilde　　II. Verey, Rosemary
635.9'0942　　SB406
ISBN 0–7011–2395–8
Printed and bound in Great Britain by
Fakenham Press Limited, Fakenham, Norfolk

CONTENTS

CONTENTS

FOREWORD

It seems to me at once rather strange and immensely flattering that a mere man has been asked to write a foreword to this book, let alone one who only discovered the art of gardening about six years ago. But then, as a contributor remarks, one of the tragedies of life is that an obsession with plants and garden planning only sets in after the age of thirty-five. Along with it, in my case, has come an interest in garden history, that much neglected field of the history of art in this country. And in that history women have always played a significant role. I see our contributors as worthy descendants of our earliest heroines of the English garden, James I's queen, Anne of Denmark, and Lucy Harington, Countess of Bedford. These were in the vanguard of the garden revolution which swept Jacobean England and their successors stretch down through Mary Capel to Gertrude Jekyll and beyond.

All garden design is an index of the ideals of the society which created them. They mirror as exactly as the other arts, the tensions and problems of an age. Four centuries later these contributors are in the vanguard of coping with the huge social revolution that has precipitated a crisis in the survival of old let alone the creation of new gardens. The Second World War was indeed a great watershed in the history of gardening in Britain. In more senses than one everything had to start again in 1945. This is the recurring theme underlying this book, the restoration of the pleasure garden after the War, a story of re-creation and retrenchment to meet the limitations and mechanization of a new era. Just as Elizabeth David's cookery books heralded the arrival of the lady of the house in the kitchen with a consequent vast improvement in the standard of cuisine, so the disappearance of gardeners as a fact of life caused an equal change within that domain. Gardens can no longer rely on armies of labour and this sadly means the end for ever of some forms of the art but yet the birth of new ones. An undoubted bonus is that gardens have become more personal than ever before. Whatever the degree of help left, there are few contributors whose hands are not constantly deep in the soil or wielding the pruning shears. The result is gardens which have the intimacy of a diary or memoir, indeed the accounts by the contributors often read like leaves torn from a journal, full of passion and idiosyncrasy as their pride and prejudice are revealed. These are private arcadias into which we, the public, are now allowed to pry. How generous they are to unfold the pages for our contemplation. How much one understands the contributor who unashamedly states that the essence of her garden is that it is a closed world.

The art of the garden, like the other arts, goes back in order to go forward. This book would provide little evidence of a return to the landscape style of Brown or Repton. There is instead a preoccupation with the formal style as it existed on either side of the age of *le jardin anglais*, the traditions of Tudor and Stuart gardening and those of its revival from the romantic era onwards, in which the architectural approach of the earlier period was married to the profusion of the cottage garden. It is significant that more contributors refer to Sissinghurst and Hidcote than to any other garden. And how much more powerful must their influence be in an age of colour lithography, of television and of the garden open to the public. Of the writers and designers who have influenced them most we are given an admirable list: William Robinson, Gertrude Jekyll, Vita Sackville-West, Graham Thomas, Margery Fish, Russell Page, Lanning Roper and Christopher Lloyd. And where would any of them be without those never-ending pilgrimages to the fortnightly shows of the R.H.S.?

Perhaps one senses above all the end of one era and the beginning of another. With unprecedented inflation and the disappearance of the last of the gardeners within the old tradition (their age is frequently dwelt upon) one speculates as to what the future may hold. If the new generation has as much drive, enthusiasm, resilience and dedication as these Englishwomen the future of that most purely patriotic of all our art forms, the garden, may rest assured.

Roy Strong
January 1979

PREFACE

When the idea of this book was first suggested to me my immediate response was, 'No, it won't work.' How on earth, I thought, could a good book emerge, compiled mostly by amateur writers? However, albeit with misgiving, I agreed to go ahead. As things have turned out I am happy to admit that I was totally wrong. The contributions are always informative, stimulating and original.

I asked Rosemary Verey if she would be willing to join me as co-editor. Fortunately for me she accepted since, without her patience, her industry, and above all her botanical knowledge, the book would never have become the worthwhile volume it is.

Some people may question the title. Why women? The answer is that all through the ages there have been dedicated women gardeners in our country, and there are perhaps more today than ever before. As far back as the seventeenth century Mary Capel, first Duchess of Beaufort, became deeply interested in horticulture. She had orangeries and greenhouses built at Badminton and in London to house the more exotic plants which were mostly new to this country and which she had recorded in two beautifully illustrated volumes. We have reproduced here two pages of the *Primulaceae* family as end-papers, and would like to take the opportunity of thanking His Grace the Duke of Beaufort for his generosity in allowing us to do so. Nearer our own time there have been many famous plants-women – Jane Loudon, Alicia Amherst, Ellen Willmott, Gertrude Jekyll and Marianne North in the nineteenth century; and Vita Sackville-West and Margery Fish in this century, to name but a few of those who have left their mark.

Historically, it is more often than not men who have done the initial planning and layout of gardens. But many women have spent endless days, months and years working in them. It is they who cosset and fuss over the plants as though they were deeply loved children. They devote hours to reading garden books and catalogues, going to shows and other people's gardens, in order to improve their knowledge and beautify still further their creations. In fact gardening often becomes an obsession with them.

We have endeavoured to be eclectic in our choice of gardens and have covered a wide area of the country, taking in both great and modest ones. We were unable to resist the temptation to go over the Border and include two highly interesting Scottish gardens. Sadly, for reasons of space, there have had to be many omissions.

As the contributions began to arrive we were amazed by their diversity. There is the article of the specialist who is not interested in a general effect but only in growing plants which she may have collected from remote parts of the world. She looks closely into every flower. Then there is the lover of form and colour; and her whose speciality is perhaps foliage plants. There is also the owner of the very

13

large garden with herbaceous borders, shrubs, trees, and literally thousands of plants, which she may have inherited, and has to modify to suit present-day conditions. One thing all the contributors have in common is unerring taste, and I need hardly say that the length of the articles bears no relation to the merits of the gardens described.

Each writer has revealed how her garden evolved, and how against mounting odds it is kept going. Anyone who owns anything over half an acre today is finding it increasingly difficult to maintain. All too often the owner is forced to reduce some part of it by putting it down to grass. Gradually many lovely gardens are shrinking, and may well end up like the dodo.

However, at the present time there are still a large number which their owners are usually willing to show to other enthusiasts. Gardeners are a generous race, not only in helping beginners with ideas and information, but in giving away plants, and many charities benefit very considerably each year from their tireless efforts. The dates and times of opening can be found in up-to-date annual lists such as the National Garden Scheme's yellow book, the Gardeners' Royal Benevolent Society's green book and *Historical Houses, Castles and Gardens in Great Britain*.

Finally, both Rosemary Verey and I would like to say how grateful we are to Dick Robinson, how enormously we have enjoyed working with the contributors and how much we ourselves have learned during the process.

Alvilde Lees-Milne

Acknowledgements

All the photographs in this book were taken by R. H. M. Robinson of the Harry Smith Horticultural Photographic Collection with the exception of the following: 3, 4, 5, 6 Grace Woodbridge; 7, 8, 48 Harry Smith; 25, 63, 73, 74, 75, 84, 87, 89, 117, 118, 119, 153, 157, 170, 182, 188, 189, 190, 191, 192 Sheila Orme/Smith Collection; 46, 47, 106, 107, 108 Anthony Huxley/Smith Collection; 116 Nancy Mary Goodall/Smith Collection; end-papers, 176 Angelo Hornak; frontispiece, 184, 186 Kenneth Scowen.

The drawings at the openings of the articles are by Davina Wynne-Jones of Gryffon Publications (pp. 15, 31, 35, 47, 52, 63, 80, 81, 106, 131, 134, 149), Laurie Clark (pp. 20, 26, 41, 45, 56, 67, 72, 78, 84, 88, 101, 116, 125, 139, 144, 146) and Cecilia Humphrys (pp. 61, 86, 92, 97, 111, 113, 122).

The endpapers are reproduced by kind permission of His Grace the Duke of Beaufort from *A Book of Botanical Drawings* executed by Daniel Frankon for the first Duchess of Beaufort in the seventeenth century.

West Wood, Walberswick, Suffolk

Miss Mea Allan's Garden

IN WRITING about the garden here I find it difficult to call it *my* garden. Too much of other people's planning and planting have gone into its making, and I grudge its earlier creators not a whit of praise for the green architecture of its bones; and for their imaginative use in walls, pillars and paving of the flint pebbles deposited here as débris by the Great Eastern glacier.

True, it is mine by choice of inheritance. Mine, too, for love of its every inch and corner. In another way I have made it mine, by piecing together its history, which otherwise would have been lost, and recently I have added a new dimension. The garden itself inspired me, telling its own history through the plants growing in it. All that was needed was the eye to read the history. Fortune and a series of wondrous coincidences gave me that eye.

When my father bought the garden (the cottage that went with it was to him incidental) it was a wilderness of weeds resulting from years of neglect during World War II. But when we learnt that the previous owner had been 'a great gardener', we came cautiously to the task of removing the weeds, for surely beneath the mass of tangling, strangling vegetation there must be some floral treasures.

And so it proved. When the mountains of ivy were piled on the bonfire, with the miles of trailing brambles, the barrowloads of ground elder, couch grass and other tormentors, the garden made by Arthur Dacres Rendall began to emerge in rare, pencil-thin, white colchicums, stunning pink *Crinum* lilies, and delicate bicoloured martagons. There was a plantain lily with enormous leaves and blackish flowers, a twenty-feet-tall strawberry tree, a rose nobody could name . . . Paved paths came to light

1 A paved path at West Wood. When Mea Allan took over the garden in 1947 it was overgrown. 'Paved paths came to light beneath a layer of weeds, which were rolled up like a stair carpet.' The garden was already divided into small garden rooms by yew hedges, rose screens and flint walls

beneath weeds we rolled up like a stair carpet. A pergola sprang into view when an arras of old man's beard was wrenched down. Finally the design of the garden was revealed.

In shape it was a long wedge formed by two converging roads. Hedges, triple-banked, cut it off from public view. Within its secret confines a path ran round the perimeter, while other paths – hidden between or behind our yew hedges, climbing-rose screens, or flint wall – divided the whole into even more secret, smaller gardens. It had a bit of everything: a rose garden, a sunken garden with a pool, a pleached alley bordering the length of the tennis lawn, mulberries, medlars, apples and plums, and a kitchen garden which was far too large. At the apex of the triangle was a collection of fine trees we referred to as 'the woody bit'.

It was one of these trees that gave me a clue to the identity of the seventeenth-century owners of the garden. Meanwhile, the plans accompanying the deeds showed how from 1891 Arthur Rendall had added pightles and parcels of land to his original cottage plot. By 1912 its layout of herbaceous borders, herb garden, pools and pathways, seats and rockery, was so interesting that Gertrude Jekyll wrote about it in her *Gardens for Small Country Houses*. The designer was a young architect suitably named A. Winter Rose, a plaque in the church records his death in the 1914–18 war. But it was sheer coincidence that in 1976, when St. Andrew's was being repaired, we learnt from the church architect that Arthur Rendall had been employed by the same firm to which young Algernon Rose was articled. Correspondence revealed that Arthur Rendall became the first secretary of the Imperial Arts League, now the Artists' League of Great Britain. 'A staunch friend to all artists, a man of intense kindness and intrepid courage, his passing means a great loss to the world of Art.'

The history of the garden assembled itself erratically like a jigsaw puzzle; here a piece, there a piece. In 1964 my biography of *The Tradescants: their Plants, Gardens and Museum, 1570–1662* was published, itself the result of a coincidence when a London friend driving through Lambeth discovered Walberswick Street, the name of my Suffolk village.

What was an East Anglian village doing in London? The then London County Council's street-naming department bade me consult the *Dictionary of National Biography* under the name Tradescant. I read that John Tradescant and his son John were gardeners to Charles I and his 'Rose and Lily Queen', Henrietta Maria of France. They had also been plant hunters, travelling the world in search of new exotics to enrich our gardens, and introducing many of our best-known and best-loved flowers. They were commemorated in the genus *Tradescantia* which gave us Moses-in-the-bulrushes for our borders and wandering sailor for our window-sills. They had left legacies to their kinsmen

2 *A hedge of the climbing rose 'Albertine' covers an iron fence that runs along the front of the house screening it from the road*

3 Looking across the sunken garden towards the 15th-century church. It is here that Mea Allan grows alpines and bulbs

Robert and Thomas Tradescant of Walberswick in Suffolk 'in remembrance of my love . . .'.

This last intriguing fact was the starting-point for six years of research that became more and more exciting. I rushed across the road to the church where, fortuitously, the seventeenth-century registers were still unremoved to the county archives; the names Robert Tradescant and Thomas Tradescant leapt from the parchment pages. A study of Court Barons and terriers revealed that Robert and Thomas were in the habit of lending money against security of land. Inevitably, it seemed, the borrowers defaulted and Robert and Thomas collected. While no vast acres were involved, the parcels, pightles and closes of land all added up. Could one of the pightles be ours?

St. Andrew's church was built in the fifteenth century. What a pity that the seventeenth-century surveyors did not take its sturdy tower as the focal point from which to measure and so plot a site described. Then we could be sure that a certain messuage and curtilage awarded to Robert Tredeskyn was in fact part of our present garden. What did prove this almost beyond doubt was the wild olive tree which the Tradescants were growing in the Lambeth nursery-garden in 1634 and which we discovered was growing in our own garden, a glory of narrow silvery leaves and pale yellow racemes wafting a scent of lemon verbena. Its botanical name is *Elaeagnus angustifolia*. Visiting botanists put its age at three hundred years old.

The Tradescants' 1634 and 1656 garden lists provided other clues. There was the elder John's 'unsavory yellow Italian Jasmine' (meaning scentless) growing here against a flint wall, the *Lysimachia vulgaris* he brought from Russia in 1618, and 'Tradescant's great rose daffodill', identified by an illustration in John Parkinson's *Paradisi in sole, paradisus terrestris*. Unmistakably, here it was at the end of March, in all its beauty of rows upon rows of petals and sepals making a lake of gold in what we call the big border, with John's Mediterranean celandine of big waxy yellow flowers spread in a carpet beneath. The daffodil is no longer in commerce and develops only from the clone, meaning that it too may have been here for three hundred years and come straight from the Lambeth nursery. Certainly Arthur Rendall would never have discarded such a beauty.

It was Arthur Rendall who laid out the rest of the garden after the end of 1913 when he acquired

17

4 Tradescant's 'great rose daffodill', first illustrated in John Parkinson's Paradisi in sole in 1629, in late March. (Right) 5 E. A. Bowles's golden sedge in front of a group of perennial candytuft

Little Church Field and the piece of land known as the Pightle. His was the framework of yew hedges enclosing 'garden rooms', and the creation of six different levels in the sunken garden by digging out a deep hole for the pond and piling the soil backwards in a series of small terraces. His touches were original, sometimes daring. Would you expect a tender shrub like *Carpenteria californica* to withstand the blighting east coast winds? It grows lush, even surpassing in floriferous white beauty the best specimens in its native California. An extravagant claim, but so I am told.

The turn of the century had been blessed with a flood of new plants from China, as a result of the Veitch nurseries sending young Ernest Henry Wilson to travel there as their collector. One of his finest introductions was *Rosa moyesii* of scarlet single flowers and vase-shaped hips, which he discovered in 1903. Arthur Rendall trained it to grow up a holly tree, so that sprays of it would surge through in a scarlet cascade. He planted many hollies, and up each a different rose. 'Mermaid' across the path was companion to *moyesii*, loveliest and finest of the single climbers with her shell-like flowers of a pale, clear, yellow filled with golden stamens.

I came to the garden in 1949 when even two years of holidays here and weekend commuting could not satisfy an agonizing yearning to leave Fleet Street and live here for ever. Part of the property my father bought was the end third of three cottages. This had been Arthur Rendall's studio: he was also a fine artist. In 1960, with my friend Grace Woodbridge, who had thrown in her lot with mine as co-researcher of *The Tradescants*, we bought the remaining two-thirds and knocked them all together and the two gardens into one, as it had been in the days of Arthur Rendall. Now began a new era in the garden's history. We started by introducing more of the plants discovered by the Tradescants, first removing a useless mirabelle hedge and making a *Tradescantia virginiana* border with Moses-in-the-bulrushes in blues, lilacs, pinks and even two different whites. We planted a larch to commemorate another of John the elder's discoveries in Russia. We fostered *Campanula rapunculoides* because it grew in his Lambeth garden, and we rooted layers of the younger John's Virginia creeper from the front of the house and trained them up leaning tree-trunks to hang in flaming curtains in the autumn.

My next biography was *The Hookers of Kew*, but we did not do so well with Hooker *fils*. Our soil is dry and non-acid: we can grow any of Johnny Trad's *Cistus* but not Joseph Hooker's rhododendrons.

We were in our element with *E. A. Bowles*. His red-leaved plantain, bronze-leaved violet, golden grass and golden sedge: all were colourful additions, to say nothing of his *Rheum palmatum* which threw a first-year pink flower-spike ten feet tall from its crown of bronze leaves. Bowles, like all good gardeners, was a great giver of plants; not only from generosity but as a way of ensuring the preservation of rarities if his own specimens died. He taught others to do the same, and from his friends and from friends of his friends came the bright blue periwinkle he found at La Grave, a cutting of his twisted willow, his white *Daphne mezereum* and some of his special crocuses.

We had a picnic with *Plants that Changed our Gardens*, for in this book I told the stories of seven plant hunters. Two were Peter Barr, the daffodil king and Reginald Farrer, pioneer of the natural rock garden. What we call the square rockery became the home of lovely little hoop petticoats and angel's tears. We turned the terraces of the sunken garden into a home for alpines. There were places where we could make an improvement or two. A dull privet hedge was sculpted into two graceful pillared hyperbolas with a gap between for a vista. In a blank piece of ground by the kitchen door we planted a herb garden between the spokes of an old wheel rescued from a derelict wagon at the farm, and we surrounded the wheel with heathers and hellebores for winter cheer, mindful of John Tradescant's Russian 'helebros albus enough to load a ship'.

Gardens grow, like the plants in them. They change in their growing, as owners can change. I shall hope when the last of my books is reflected here in flowers that some other gardener will pick up the green torch lit so long ago, and bear it with joy, as I do.

Mea Allan

6 *A January vista: snow emphasizes the architectural structure of the Huntingdon elms,* Ulmus vegeta

Knightshayes Court, Tiverton, Devonshire

Lady Heathcoat Amory's Garden

WHEN MY husband and I married in 1937, we inherited a large Victorian house, with a fine view over a park framed by forest trees, and the rolling Devon hills beyond. The setting of the house was fortunate, situated four hundred feet above sea-level, surrounded by wild woodland – beech, birch, chestnut, lime and oak, and a magnificent stand of Douglas firs overlooking the back drive. Regrettably many of the fine old trees have now died, either from elm disease or as a consequence of the 1976 drought which was disastrous for the beech and birch trees.

It had certainly never crossed our minds that mature trees could vanish almost overnight, and we had not made a regular practice of planting up young forest trees. Quite rightly, tree planting is now recognized as a duty for the sake of future generations and it is a comfort to know that visitors will one day enjoy the fruits of the consecutive planting which is being carried out by the National Trust, who took over the property when my husband died in 1972.

In 1937 the scope of the garden was confined to a few formal terraces, some bedding out, a

7 *An alpine border at Knightshayes. The stone steps lead to the paved garden. (See plate 10)*

8 *The woodland garden in spring, showing an interesting mixture of plants and mature trees*

9 *The terrace, looking from the woodland garden towards the house.*
Knightshayes, built by William Burges in about 1870, commands a fine view over
the park to the river Exe and the rolling Devon hills

tortuously clipped yew topiary and a small paved area with rose beds. The rest was given over to a bowling green and a large expanse of lawn. In short, we were the owners of a typical Victorian garden. The potential for change was enormous, and in my initial burst of enthusiasm I rushed headlong into making a new rose garden (which, unknowingly, I sited in the wrong position) and dotting around a few shrubs. Then the war came and our energies were directed elsewhere.

In 1946 we began to plan the garden in earnest, and fortunately we were able to call upon the advice of a splendid old lady, Miss Nellie Britton, who ran a rock garden nursery near Tiverton. She made us aware of the detail in the smallest plants, and we became conscious for the first time of the perfection of the tiniest petal. I can remember her concern when Jack became excited by magnolias and rhododendrons as she felt he might neglect rock plants for ever. But right from the start we admired the biggest and the smallest of blooms, and this diversity helped us to create a garden based on plants of any size or kind that appealed to us. Knightshayes has never been a specialist garden containing a comprehensive collection of a few species, but rather a nursery for the plants we fell in love with.

We began near the house, loosening the appearance of the stiff formal terraces with small shrubs, roses and plants. In the paved garden we replaced the roses with low carpeting plants, whose grey leaves and delicate colours spread over the flagstones. High yew topiary hedges surrounded this garden as well as the adjacent bowling green which was subsequently sacrificed to make way for a pool with a statue, stone benches and a weeping pear, which was induced to hang over the pool, and

21

pruned regularly every year to keep its form light and thin. The atmosphere is peaceful and still, in sharp contrast to the busy alpine border and other distractions outside.

It is difficult to remember changes in their right order. But it is not difficult to remember the friends who over the years have helped us with suggestions, comments and generous gifts of plants. To mention only two, Graham Thomas and Lanning Roper visited us many times, and to our delight accepted us as fellow gardeners.

Sir Eric Savill, who is such an inspiring and encouraging enthusiast, was a tremendous support when we decided to break new ground and extend the garden into the wood beyond the terraces, and 'the garden in the wood' became the most enthralling adventure of all. After the war Jack soon became a keen collector of plants. I was particularly interested in placing and arranging these in the context of the big trees we had left standing, having cut down many hundreds of the smaller ones.

Having removed the boundary fence line out of sight, we brought into the garden, each year, a piece of woodland approximately the size of a tennis court. Later, when with the help of more modern machinery we were clearing bigger slices among the remaining trees, the realization came that with terraces, lawns and borders twenty-five acres was more than enough to cope with. But temptation always dwelt just beyond the fence which was pushed back many times.

In 1963 we were joined by Michael Hickson as a very young head gardener, full of enthusiasm, and at the same time talented and efficient. His help and devotion to the garden, which has been so appreciated by us, has led to one scheme after another and also, we are sure, to the enhanced enjoyment of thousands of visitors.

The garden certainly did not grow from a drawing board. Ideas came, and proved their worth by trial and error. You cannot really foresee how a garden will develop or what it will look like over a period of about thirty years. I think we realized fairly soon that a garden does not stand still. It either improves or regresses. A certain ruthlessness is necessary, particularly when combating the common error of overcrowding. One is either pulling out or putting in plants, as well as altering the sizes and shapes of borders and glades.

More than once I have been asked whether books have helped in making the garden. Certainly one, written many years ago by Miss Sylvia Crowe, had a great influence. She pointed out how often our beautiful English countryside is spoilt by gardens blazing in colour, which intrude on a natural backdrop of fields and distances. My rose garden had to face this criticism. A lovely vista from the terrace in front of the house stretches away on a slight slope through the park. In the lower foreground of this is a broad grass terrace retaining narrow paving and beds in the Victorian style. And this was the site I selected for my first attempt at a rose garden. I was later shaken by the realization that the view had been interrupted and the eye distracted. In trying to tone down the disparity, the red roses were changed to cream and soft magenta ones, in imitation of the colour of our wild flowers. However the effect still jarred, and the problem was not resolved until the rose beds had been flattened and grassed over. The remaining rose beds at either end of the terrace were converted into two flat patchwork circles of scented thyme, each with a stone ornament. Only one original feature was retained, a low fountain of lead dolphins with a single spout to give that enchanting musical sound of splashing water. The transformation was complete and ever since the flowering colours at Knightshayes have been kept on the cool side.

The main object of all our efforts was to introduce new vistas, never if possible to repeat former plantings, and to give unexpected pleasure at the turning of corners. For instance, one surprise which has been effective is to find, on entering a secluded and shady glade ostensibly planted out with a few unusual shrubs, a spring carpet of yellow, pink and white dogtooth violets on a backcloth of green moss. Elsewhere, beneath very high Douglas firs, the ground is covered with varying shades of blue and green prostrate conifers intermingled with autumn and winter cyclamen.

In other places, low peat walls have been built to enclose and provide safe areas for small plants, so that they do not become lost and overshadowed by larger shrubs. It has been our aim to create a continuous and unexpected combination of flowers and foliage throughout the spring, summer and autumn. A garden need never have an off season, particularly if the beauty and contrasts of evergreen foliage are understood and not forgotten. A rule we have always kept, which is I think a good one, is

10 Low carpeting plants, whose grey leaves and delicate colours spread over the flagstones, have replaced roses. This garden is surrounded by high topiary hedges

that if a group of plants is continually passed, or bypassed without being looked at, then this area is obviously dull and must be altered to attract attention.

The last enterprise my husband and I undertook together was to make a willow garden in a neglected fold in the ground to the west of the main drive, where a slope leads to our only small piece of spring water. We uprooted a forest of *Rhododendron ponticum* from this shallow valley, but were careful to retain the clumps of old fashioned Ghent azaleas. We then introduced a variety of willows, arresting with their coloured stems, as well as catkins and summer foliage.

Since I am describing the making of the garden I have purposely avoided introducing nomenclature and listing plants. To mention only a few would be misleading as the garden is packed with many varieties. At the same time we have always been concerned with leaving open areas of grass in the wood. This, as plantsmen will realize, requires a great deal of self-discipline! Yet a garden can often become too profuse to digest unless there are intervals in it wherein the mind can relax.

The designing and tending of a garden becomes, as all true gardeners know, the obsession of a lifetime; but the form it takes, and how one enjoys it, can differ greatly. There are those gardeners who like to work on the ground with their hands, and this was our way. For years, until Michael joined us,

11 Two of the groups of rhododendrons in a sunlit clearing: Rh. augustinii *and*
Rh. yunnanense

12 *An* urn *of* Zauschneria cana *is surrounded by silver and variegated plants* (left)
13 *White* Olearia cheesemanii (rani) *and* Rhododendron *'Tally-Ho' in the woodland garden* (centre)
14 *A border with* Allium albo-pilosum, Tropaeolum polyphyllum *and* Alstroemeria *'Ligtu hybrids'* (right)

Jack and I planted, propagated and tended everything that two pairs of hands could manage, with help only for the rougher work. Jack enormously enjoyed telling non-gardeners that gardening was, 'Eleven months of hard labour, and one month of acute disappointment'. But he did not really mean it!

It seems to me that the prime objective of a gardener is to show off plants, and certainly this was our sole reason for making a garden. Plants can create peace and contentment, and the opening of a flower and the ripening of a berry can stir the emotions to the full. I think that the thrill of gardening lies in the absorbing interest that the growth and change in the lives of plants holds for us. There are days in early spring when the ground seems almost to be moving, with green tips forcing themselves up to the light, and one can only stand back and watch with wonder the innate vitality of plants, in which one has no part other than in the creation of a worthy home for them. I cannot express the joy we felt, years ago, when for the first time one of our plants was accepted by a very well-known plantsman whose garden was widely and affectionately known as a 'jungle of gems'.

Other memories spring to mind. The bite of anticipation as we embarked on one of our many projects, the haunting scent of bonfires, or the crash of felled trees in the wood. To some this seemed wantonly destructive, but it was necessary, as it gave light and space to the remaining trees which then grew into vigorous and outstanding specimens.

Gardening has been full of excitement for me. Although the joy and adventures I shared in laying out a garden can never fade, I know at heart I am a plantswoman, and in company with all those who are devoted to horticulture, Knightshayes has been for me, a constant source of delight. I hope it will continue to give pleasure to those who come to see a rare or unusual plant, or simply to enjoy the surroundings.

Joyce Heathcoat Amory.

Arley Hall, Northwich, Cheshire

The Viscountess Ashbrook's Garden

IN 1939 my husband and I became responsible for a large country house garden, which until then had absorbed the labour of at least six gardeners. It was a very old garden and had been greatly loved by many generations of my family. During the war years we managed somehow to preserve it, but by 1945 it was in pretty bad shape. We could not bear to abandon it, but equally it was out of the question to restore and maintain its pre-war condition for the sole enjoyment of our own family.

For some years we ran part of it as a market garden, but this became increasingly unrewarding. In 1960, to my enormous relief, we decided to discontinue marketing and made plans to open the garden to the public. We hoped thereby to produce an income to help pay the maintenance expenses, and also, by sharing it with other people, to justify our wish to preserve it.

There has probably been a garden on this site since the first house was built at Arley by my forbears five hundred years ago, but it was my great-grandparents who, early in the last century, laid the foundations of the present design. They separated the garden from the park by a ha-ha, creating a terrace two hundred and twenty yards long, which leads to a rock and water dell where they made an alpine garden. This terrace, together with a double herbaceous border, an avenue of fourteen evergreen oaks (*Quercus ilex*) clipped to the shape of giant cylinders, and two large walled kitchen gardens, made the framework of their design. This was very formal, and the planting, which included a great deal of yew and holly topiary, was planned to provide interest in all months of the year.

My aim was to restore the garden to its pre-war standard. I knew that some simplification would be necessary, but hoped to achieve this without changing its character. In addition to the principal features already mentioned, it contains several small enclosed gardens concealed from the main vistas, which give a great sense of intimacy. As these little gardens had become badly overgrown, I decided to begin by replanting each one in turn, mistakes could then be corrected without affecting the general landscape. I made full use of this facility, for I am always loth to live with my mistakes, whether of design or plantsmanship. Frequently I find that it is well worth moving an unhappy or badly placed plant to a different site, and I never banish anything until it has sampled several choices of accommodation. We have an acid clay sub-soil which needs good drainage and soil aeration. With this proviso, we can grow a great variety of plants, but like all living things they are often unpredictable in their behaviour. I bear in mind the old adage that you should put one specimen of a plant where you think it will thrive, a second where you hope it will, and a third where you are convinced it won't. The result is often surprising.

15 One of the famous double herbaceous borders at Arley Hall. The borders are thought to be among the oldest in Britain and are shown on a plan of 1846

My first project was to improve the rock garden at the end of the terrace. It had been designed with steep banks of rocks rising from a small winding pool, but the surrounding trees – oaks, yews, hollies and the red *Acer palmatum* – now made it too shady a site for the alpine plants for which it was designed. We replaced them with the smaller species and hybrid rhododendrons, azaleas, and other flowering shrubs which settled happily amongst the rocks, although in very dry weather some of the larger-leafed rhododendrons give us anxious moments. Azaleas appear to need very little soil or moisture, and their flowers in spring and foliage in autumn reflect and enhance the brilliance of the acers. These, when seen from the pond level are high above one's head, and the light shines through their crimson leaves with a lovely translucence. In high summer this part of the garden is lush and green and great fronds of Osmunda fern fringe the pool. It is a quiet, shady place, and once or twice in the evening I have seen a kingfisher dart across the water.

It was an article by Vita Sackville-West which first drew my attention to shrub roses. We had a collection of the Hybrid Tea varieties planted in formal beds in front of a little half-timbered tea cottage. These grew only moderately well, and one fortunate day it occurred to me to see if the shrub roses would like us better. Luckily they did; in fact they like us very much, and we are devoted to them. I planted them in large irregular beds around the cottage, which is now encircled by these lovely shrubs. I think my favourites are the old-fashioned, soft-coloured pinks and purples, with evocative names like 'Souvenir de la Malmaison', 'Tour de Malakoff', 'Fantin Latour' and 'Tuscany'. But some of the modern varieties, 'Constance Spry', 'Aloha' and the golden 'Lady Sonia', are so generous in their flowering and so gay and exuberant that one cannot neglect them. But perhaps of all roses the

27

16 A spring corner, with Viburnum plicatum, Meconopsis grandis *and azaleas against a background of lime trees in the park*

17 The herb garden. Lady Ashbrook's favourite in this aromatic collection is her Eau de Cologne mint

most appealing to me is the lovely *Rosa* 'Sancta', her single flowers, whose delicate, pink petals encircle golden stamens, are an enchanting sight in June. She looks fragile but is, in fact, sturdy and trouble-free. I believe that she has an older history than any other garden rose, and was first discovered in the courtyards of Christian sanctuaries in Abyssinia.

The herbaceous border, shown on a map of 1846, must be one of the oldest in the United Kingdom. It was painted by George Elgood in 1889, and appears in a book, *Some English Gardens* produced by him and Gertrude Jekyll. It is about ninety yards long, supported on one side by a brick wall and on the other by a yew hedge. It is divided by huge buttresses of clipped yew into four beds on either side of a grass path which leads to a pavilion of classical design known as the Alcove. Many of the plants growing in it today can be seen in Elgood's painting. I have tried to preserve the old flowers as well as adding new varieties, because the former seem to suit this garden particularly well. In early June the border has its 'blue period' and I prefer this to any other season. The varied blues of *Delphinium*, *Campanula*, and 'Johnson's Blue' *Geranium* are magical against the velvety green of the young growth on the yew hedges, and for a week or two I eliminate most other colours except for pale yellow.

By July, exuberance takes over and detailed colour planning is impossible; the mellow background of wall and hedge, however, prevents any appearance of gaudiness. I am cautious with hot yellow flowers which I think can sometimes seem strident. They come into their own in late September with the heleniums, the dahlias and the solidagos, and one is grateful then for their warmth and richness.

There used to be three kitchen gardens, but in 1960 we redesigned the largest of these. Surrounded by high walls it makes a sheltered enclosure of about one and a half acres for those shrubs and small flowering trees which need protection from our all-too-frequent Cheshire winds. The middle of the garden is filled by a large lawn, intersected by two paths, one running north and south, the other east and west. They converge on a lily pond surrounded by four fastigiate beech trees, and beds of the

Floribunda rose 'Iceberg'. Mixed red roses, thickly edged with *Nepeta* are planted in the centre of the south-facing wall. Close by are *Abutilon vitifolium*, *Hoheria lyallii*, *Carpenteria californica*, and other cherished plants which need favoured treatment, for this part of the garden has a kindly soil. I hope to coax the lovely Chatham Island forget-me-not to grow here, but in spite of its name, I keep forgetting to bury fish remains around its roots to remind it of its native sea-shore.

A complete contrast in scale are two little enclosed gardens, one for herbs and the other for sweet-scented plants. The former has a large collection of herbs, most of them aromatic, amongst which I find the scent of the Eau de Cologne mint especially delicious, far superior to the bottled stuff. In the other garden I try to have scents throughout the year, which curiously is almost easier to achieve in winter than in summer. Hitherto, I have not planted the January flowering wintersweet which I think is the wickedest-looking flower I know. Its scent is heavenly, but the flowers seem to me diabolical. In midsummer I suppose lilies are without equal for fragrance and form. They are the aristocrats of the garden, but two little, old-fashioned plants, mignonette and heliotrope enchant me, and I like to grow them together in a raised bed where they can be given the extra lime which they require on our soil.

All gardeners enjoy growing something which defeats their neighbours. One of our successes is *Embothrium coccineum* which does not usually thrive in Cheshire. We planted it in the autumn of 1962 and all the pundits said we were wasting our time. It survived that brutal winter, and is now a lusty tree of twenty feet. Audacity sometimes pays! Unfortunately, my husband does not admire it, and calls it a garish status symbol, lacking real elegance. This may be partially true, but its flowers give me great satisfaction, and when in full bloom draw astonished admiration from visitors.

I much enjoy showing the garden to anyone who is genuinely interested, whether they are knowledgeable or not. But I am sure one must be wary of following advice unless it accords with one's

18 *Floribunda roses including 'Rosemary Rose', edged with nepeta, surround two stone urns under a south-facing wall*

19 *The* Quercus ilex *avenue. Fourteen evergreen oaks have been clipped to the shape of giant cylinders*

20 *The scented garden beside the 15th-century clock tower and 'the Ride'. This garden is designed to provide scents throughout the year. Pink floribunda roses are edged with dwarf lavender*

own taste. Whether this be good or bad, if a garden is to have character it must reflect an individual taste, otherwise it will be a hotch-potch without cohesion.

Long before I had any responsibility for this garden, people used to say it had a very peaceful atmosphere. I have tried hard to preserve this quality, due partly to age, and partly to the dignified simplicity of my great-grandparents' composition. Their original structure of walls, hedges and avenues provide the frame within which one can develop the picture. Unlike a painting, it is a living picture, which changes as the years pass. These changes create problems, but also challenges, and herein lies the fascination of gardening. The picture is never finished; opportunity is always there for tomorrow.

Elizabeth Ashbrook

21 *Early Dutch honeysuckle* Lonicera periclymenum *'Belgica' growing through a carpet of ladies' mantle,* Alchemilla mollis

Rodmarton Manor, Cirencester, Gloucestershire

Mrs Anthony Biddulph's Garden

MY LOVE of gardening started with a love of wild flowers. I was a wild flower enthusiast. I found 1,400 by the time I was fourteen years old. I hunted for them all over Britain and, accompanied by a bishop wearing his gaiters, even found the wild tulip. My first garden was twelve by six feet, quite beautiful with a 'Dorothy Perkins' rose and all bedding out. Then I progressed to a farm house garden which was certainly learning the hard way. A Cotswold farm does not necessarily produce a fertile soil and we were on brash, five hundred feet up. An herbaceous border and one round rose bed had to be pick-axed out. But there were compensations. *Lilium candidum* flourished beautifully every year whereas here they won't grow at all.

Coming to this very much larger garden, about seven acres in all, was a challenge. Still on brashy soil it had the bare bones of an older garden. It had originally been designed by the Barnsleys of Cotswold craftsmen fame, and friends of Sedding. When we arrived here we had to scythe along the raspberries to be able to pick them, pheasants nested in the borders, but worst of all the head gardener we had inherited would not let us into the potting-shed! Two major difficulties in the kitchen garden were a hundred and fifty unnamed apple trees and box edging everywhere, thickly growing with couch. The apples and the box edging went and the couch is going slowly.

To help with such a mammoth task, I visited other gardens and read gardening books by Jekyll, Robinson, Margery Fish and the R.H.S. *Dictionary of Gardening*. I visited the R.H.S. and Chelsea shows, as well as the Botanic Gardens in Oxford, Edinburgh and Sydney. Wisley and Kew were a delight.

We had to plan for a labour-saving garden. There would no longer be ten gardeners, but we were determined to enjoy it and based our ideas round shapes, permanent shades of colour, paving, ornaments, topiary, scents and ground cover.

We had to get machinery that really helps and consequently my best friends have become a Honda plough, a Merrytiller and a Little Wonder hedge trimmer. Grass has to be cut down, in more senses than one, and the regular weekly mow is time consuming. There is no digging except in the kitchen garden. I never use spray on the soil between shrubs or plants which would be useful for weed control; I fear unforeseen results in later years.

I decided that a terrace was essential, as well as a leisure garden, herbaceous and shrub borders, bulbs and cherry trees with species roses to follow, a wild garden and a winter garden. The garden began to be divided up into rooms. I did not copy Hidcote, Sissinghurst or Crathes, but rather followed my own inclination.

The first part to evolve was the leisure garden. The layout was formal, real stone paving mixed in places with concrete slabs, made with farm labour. Potentilla, hyssop and lavender, with a gold bed and a grey bed and ground cover. Eventually roses were allowed in and the only answer to the weed problem was to mulch and mulch again. The gold bed has *Thuja* 'Rheingold', *Elaeagnus pungens* 'Maculata', and *Taxus* 'Dovastonii Aurea'. It is never weeded and is perhaps the most successful.

I have four large herbaceous and shrub borders with a lily pond in the middle, and a charming Cotswold summer house at the end. On one side is a high wall and on the other a high yew hedge. Here the scene changes. The basic outline is recurrent, shrub roses such as *rubrifolia*, 'Penelope', 'Pax', 'Elmshorn' and hardy fuchsias, interspersed with herbaceous plants such as *Agapanthus* and various eryngiums. Colour is demanded here from June until October; alliums and *Clematis* help provide this.

I then turned my attention to the winter garden, close to the house. Facing south, no east wind could penetrate here, and existing pleached limes increased the shelter, enabling *Helleborus orientalis*, *niger*, *atrorubens*, *foetidus*, special *Galanthus*, *Magnolia grandiflora*, *Choisya*, and 'Tête-à-tête' *Narcissus* to flourish.

The terrace has topiary work, peacocks and other shapes that the yew wanted to make. There are many tubs full, literally full of bedding plants. I call it my 'Park Department'. I revel in the greys, petunias and geraniums. People are such snobs and dislike plants like *Tagetes*, which can be fascinating in the right place.

I have tried hard to make a white and grey border but somehow the plants defeat me. *Colchicum autumnale* 'Alba' are superb, as are the white *Agapanthus*. But then a beautiful pink paeony blooms. I shall call it my pastel border, and hope that no kind friend will give me a plant that turns out to be stridently coloured!

One of my favourite garden 'rooms' is the cherry orchard. It is full of bulbs in spring, and species

22 and 23 Two views of the leisure garden at Rodmarton Manor. Mrs. Biddulph finds that the gold bed never needs weeding. Well-mulched roses grow with lavender and grey plants

24 *A view from the lily pond, between the herbaceous borders, to the Cotswold summerhouse*

25 *Looking across the leisure garden towards the house, built by the Barnsley brothers between 1909 and 1926*

roses from my own cuttings in summer. There is space and tranquillity and a more planned approach to planting.

I inherited many stone troughs. They were collected by my son from around the farm, where they were no longer needed. I am no alpinist, but I pop into them all the small plants that would get lost in such a large garden, such as gentians, triteleias and *Hacquetia epipactis*.

The kitchen garden is vast, and swallows up my only available help. I would love to have a few new apple trees on dwarf rooting stock; instead, I have many old cordons which are difficult to deal with. They bear apples but not perfect ones. They should be discarded and the pears worry me even more. There are many known and unknown sorts and without exception they all fruited in the drought year of 1976. One has so much to learn about figs, peaches, nectarines and 'Morello' cherries.

My real joy is my mist-propagator in one of the old greenhouses. In here go cuttings at all times of the year. Some take and some do not. It is a fascinating part of gardening. The mist is temperamental because of our limey water, but works when coaxed.

A garden is always changing. As a shrub grows and mingles with its neighbours the original scheme alters. One must also be firm and discard and move plants. I grew a *Ginkgo biloba* from a cutting and it looked sick and sorry. After being moved into another part of the garden it is thriving. My most architectural plant was *Heracleum mantegazzianum*, with giant leaves and vast umbel flowers. It was terrific and much admired. But when the seeds came up everywhere with a long root it had to go. I cannot face it yet even in the wild part of the garden. Its skin blistering capabilities are another worry.

26 *Some of the stone troughs collected on the estate, in which many alpine treasures are kept*

27 *Yew hedges are a feature of this garden. Here they are photographed in the spring*

I am a great believer in planting out of the wind. So much cannot survive the east wind in February and March. *Eucryphia* 'Nymansay' survived the drought, but was killed by the wind.

I have snowdrop-mania and have *Galanthus elwesii, atkinsii, nivalis reginae-olgae* and *n. scharlokii*. I would go miles to see a new specimen. I also have a great interest in hollies and ivies. They are a vast subject. I like most variegated plants, aucubas, variegated phormiums. They create light and shade in the garden. Variegated hostas give me a pleasure that cannot be described.

My real dislike is this craze for growing climbing plants up old apple trees. The first year a clematis looks ethereal but wait five years and it looks like a disembowelled mattress (as Christopher Lloyd said about an unpruned clematis) or you have a dead apple tree. I am also beginning to dislike or rather fear the lamiums. They are wonderful for keeping a garden clean after clearing operations, but they begin to invade, do not stop invading and are very hard work indeed to eradicate. They are only suitable for a wild garden where they cannot smother your special plants.

I love showing friends and acquaintances round my garden. There is so much to learn and exchange from other enthusiasts. At the end of one and a half hours the non-keen gardener does not come again!

All plants must be labelled and labelled properly. I have tried indelible inks, good for six or eight years, but sooner or later labels just disappear or are illegible. After having forty-eight cows with one bull in my garden I was given a real labelling machine as a peace offering. The labels are black and strong and everlasting. I am sure that more plants are lost by being dug up in the winter when they are underground than by any other cause. A label is a must for a genuine gardener.

Mary D Biddulph

Kiftsgate Court, Campden, Gloucestershire

Mrs D. H. Binny's Garden

HOW EXCITING to have a ruin, a grand ruin complete with Palladian portico in the middle of the garden. It would be so easy to take the roof off Kiftsgate, allowing the yellow *banksian* rose to weep over the top and perhaps meet up inside with the wisteria. No longer would one have to cut the huge leaved *Magnolia delavayi* away from the windows, and perhaps, as Miss Coxhead said in the R.H.S. *Journal*, the 'Kiftsgate' rose would seize its chance to overpower all around and cover the ramparts of a Sleeping Beauty palace. I know I will never dismantle the house as it still means too much to me. There are too many happy memories, of my own childhood and those spent with my family, for me to destroy it, the beautiful polished floors, the lingering smell of wood smoke, the 'art deco' dining-room and the colourful flower mural by Lawrence Johnston of Hidcote fame.

My mother, Heather Muir, was a very creative and modern woman for her time, and although there is no doubt that Lawrence Johnston, a life long friend, helped her with the design of her house and garden, it was her own great colour sense and love of plants that produced the final results in the garden, I think she must have been one of the first gardeners to keep borders to definite tones of colour as with the pink, crimson, lavender, purple and abundant greys of the 'wide border', then the dark mahogany foliage coupled with golden and sulphur yellows, splashed with vivid blues and mauves of the 'yellow border'. A. G. L. Hellyer said in the magazine *Amateur Gardening*, 'The purpose is to produce a series of pictures in colour that are rich but never glaring. They are the colours I associate with fine old tapestry.' These colour schemes are the same to this day, although many of the plants have changed.

My parents bought Kiftsgate in 1918 and over the next thirty years the garden developed from nothing. Luckily the limes down the drive, the Scots firs edging the escarpment and the great elm avenue, leading

28 The 'Rosa Mundi' hedges at Kiftsgate, planted in 1928

from Mickleton church below, were planted in 1750. It was not until 1890 that the family in Mickleton Manor decided to take advantage of these trees, and the magnificent views, and built Kiftsgate, complete with a Georgian portico, transported from their old home.

In 1954 I inherited a mature garden. There was however a snag, it was difficult to change things and in fact it took me four years to pluck up enough self-confidence to alter my mother's plans, but I realized finally that gardens, like time, do not stand still and once I had started to implant my own ideas, there was no turning back. The swimming-pool was the first big project, shaped as a half moon and sited on the lower lawn. It had to be made to fit in with the surrounding garden with a natural stone edge. To the builders' dismay there were no blue tiles or diving-boards.

The grey foliage border is probably the best new creation I have achieved. A dirty grass slope facing north made an unpromising situation. Along it a low containing wall was built by an Italian gardener we had at the time, but when we started to cultivate it my heart sank, as the soil turned out to be solid yellow clay, obviously the house foundations had been dumped there! However, by this time I was determined to succeed, so contrary to all rules it was lightly forked over with a lot of very coarse peat spread on top. This has proved fairly successful although even now when a new hole is dug the yellow clay is very much in evidence. Planting was exciting, it was the first time I had made a border from scratch. I decided to have entirely silver and grey foliage with some white flowering plants. This has been adhered to although the first plan was altered considerably, plants are inclined not to grow just as you expect! The *Eucalyptus gunnii* has become a tree and dominates the border. The two *Elaeagnus × ebbingei* outgrew their station and have been removed. Luckily we were able to transplant the grey blue *Juniperus squamata* 'Meyeri' to another part of the border as it was being swamped by the eucalyptus. This grey border was a godsend during the appalling drought of 1976. It was the one part of the garden that continued to look reasonably healthy.

I spend many happy and contented hours gardening on my own, stopping now and then to relax with a cigarella, or perhaps to walk around with my talented head gardener David Weller, discussing ideas and planning the future. There is always so much that requires attention with only David and his pleasant helper Steve Gibson to do it all, as well as propagating the many plants we sell on open days. During these promenades I happily suggest to David the most difficult subjects for cuttings and leave him to work out the problems involved. When Michael Hickson from Knightshayes visited Kiftsgate he was most helpful in showing us how to take cuttings of my favourite plant *Carpenteria californica*. We now have a fair number of successes with this temperamental shrub. Mr. Percy Picton explained how he takes tree paeony cuttings, so I am keeping my fingers crossed that David will manage to propagate *Paeonia suffruticosa* 'Rock's variety' which has enormous white single flowers splashed with maroon centres. Propagating our own plants is a tremendous help and I do not feel so extravagant using them to fill in gaps in the spring. I still do my main order for new material in the autumn, having collected names and thought about where each plant will go during the summer months. Sometimes I am tempted to buy a plant on impulse, but I do not think it is a good idea to have to find a place for a plant one has bought, much better to buy a plant for the place.

Nearly all my gardening has been learnt from experience, sometimes bitter, as when a heavy dressing of hop manure was put on a steep bank: it dried out during the summer and ninety per cent finished on the path below. I visit as many gardens as possible each summer getting new ideas and seeing many plants I do not know. I shall never forget the purple *Cotinus coggygria* growing against a

29 *The wide border, in which the mixture of colour with abundant greys creates
effects that are rich but never glaring, reminiscent of fine old tapestry*

37

30 Clematis viticella *'Abundance' below the house*

31 *Lavender,* Allium albo-pilosum *and* A. cernuum

grey background of *Pyrus salicifolia* at Newby. It is a colour combination I have since used, although not with the same plants.

I dislike those regimented tiered up clumps of plants with a jumble of colour which is often found in a herbaceous border. 'Ground cover' I consider a disaster word, a labyrinth of *Lamium*, a potage of *Vinca* creeping into everything, causing endless work and destruction and making forking over and feeding a lost battle. However, having said this, I must confess we do use ground cover plants where nothing else will grow, and one of the most successful plantings is a solid block of *Campanula latiloba* growing in deep shade on a dry inhospitable bank. Another of my 'hates' is to see clematis growing through shrubs or roses so spoiling the beauty both of themselves and their hosts en route.

There is no herb garden at Kiftsgate although I can see their fascination. The wide border has a bay tree, this makes a good wind break, whilst the yellow *Origanum* and *Melissa* have always been used as decorative plants in the garden; rosemary grows well on the dry banks so the kitchen is provided for. I returned from seeing the wonderfully laid out formal vegetable garden at Villandry determined to have one here. Those matching triangles of purple cabbage, laced by blue-green leeks, and clumps of globe artichokes ringed by bright green parsley made a marvellously satisfactory design and colour scheme. On reflection I realized it would mean employing another gardener and was therefore impracticable. The walled kitchen-garden is now planted with a hundred *Eucalyptus gunnii*.

My advice (for what it is worth!) to anybody starting a new garden is to spend at least a year assessing where the main blast of wind comes from, where there is a frost pocket and what will grow in your soil. So often hedges and wind breaks are put in the wrong places and expensive plants where they have no chance of surviving. I would dearly love to grow camellias and have wasted time and money planting them to no avail. During your first year a good start can be made getting rid of the weeds, listening to advice from your friends (although not always following it!), and above all

38

deciding on colour schemes and drawing up plans, which I hope will include keeping the existing trees, so often cut down and deeply mourned at a later date.

I realize that most gardens these days are small with little or no help available so I would suggest you start your border by planting various shrubs. Choose them for size and colour to suit your site and general scheme and allow them space to grow to their natural sizes so that pruning into ugly lumps is unnecessary. To me all pruning should be done with a definite object in view, either to help produce strong new growth by taking away the weak straggly pieces, as with Floribunda roses, deutzias and summer flowering *Ceanothus*, or because the subject is growing into and killing a neighbour. Even this advice has to be treated with caution as so often plants intermingling produce a wonderful effect. To return to your border, around your skeleton shrubs I would suggest putting in expendable plants to be removed as your shrubs grow, and planting the more or less permanent herbaceous ones in drifts of four or five with perhaps a couple further away to carry your eye on, and not in those tight little clumps. I am not at all afraid of putting in one plant by itself. My sister's small and charming garden is full of 'oners'! I feel another important point is to break away from graduated heights; something tall in front will break the monotony and make a secret inlet beyond it.

I do most of the weeding at Kiftsgate with the help of Mrs. Warren who works hard for a certain number of hours each week. I leave the desperately steep, pine needle covered banks to my gardeners' agile young limbs. My children love to photograph my behind in the air as I bend over, endlessly pulling weeds as I go. No weedkillers are used on the borders which is probably why we get many interesting rose seedlings. A half child of *R. filipes* 'Kiftsgate' has seeded on a dirty north bank, and with all the vigour of its parent it is quickly taking over. The young foliage is bronze-red and it carries panicles of sweetly scented white flowers. After a lot of discussion it has been named 'Diany Binny'. I

32 The lower garden. A mixture of roses, shrubs and ground-cover plants. (Right) *33 Early autumn. Luxuriant planting in tones of greys and mauves flanks the path leading to the house. Here a superb specimen of* Hydrangea villosa *grows against the mellow Cotswold stone*

34 *A fine planting of* Cyclamen hederaefolium *on the way to the lower garden*

35 Clematis alpina *cascading down the steps near the house*

was keen on 'Old Ma Bin' which many of my friends call me. In 1970 there was a disaster when a hormone poison spray used on the farm land below rose owing to the exceptionally hot weather, and drifted over the garden, the result being that plants grew in distorted shapes with no flowers. I had been away and almost wept when I returned and saw the damage. Fortunately most things had recovered by the following year.

I can state unequivocally that I would hate not to open the garden as we now do. Apart from the financial help it means it has to be kept reasonably tidy, properly weeded, and staked where necessary. Best of all you meet and talk to so many interesting people and keen gardeners. Certainly no gardening is possible on open days. David and Steve retire to the kitchen garden whilst I sit at the entrance selling tickets and plants, advising, listening and learning, and enjoying it all enormously.

Diany Binng

36 *Part of the famous* R. filipes *'Kiftsgate', which climbs and spreads over a wide area*

37 *The terrace at the front of the house. Old fashioned roses grow in box-edged beds*

Ince Castle, Saltash, Cornwall

The Viscountess Boyd of Merton's Garden

WHEN WE bought this seventeenth-century manor house in south-east Cornwall seventeen years ago our first task was to restore it. Meanwhile we began to discover a little about local gardening conditions. We had a lot to learn. Our first shock was the almost terrifying strength of the wind, which, coupled with the lack of topsoil – in some places the shale is only a few inches below the surface – remains our worst enemy. Another surprise was that this resulted in a very dry garden. Our rainfall is not above average and the shale drains the water away in no time at all. In fact most Mediterranean plants flourish here, particularly those with grey leaves.

The previous owners were not gardeners. We found six *Magnolia grandiflora* growing against the house. (They are still there. Who could wilfully destroy a well-grown magnolia?) There was a patch of garden on the south side and another smaller one to the east. In a spinney, planted over a hundred years ago to protect the house from the gales, daffodils were naturalized and a small walled garden was full of ancient diseased Hybrid Tea roses. This, apart from the kitchen garden and orchard, completed the picture.

I must explain that the house stands high on a peninsula jutting out into the Lynher estuary with a beautiful view of the river to the south and east. On the south side, where the existing patch of garden was bounded by lovely stone walls, we decided to make a

38 Cobbled paths in the pink and grey garden at Ince Castle

formal garden on two levels. On the higher level we put down paving in front of the house, kept the small lawn, and re-built the raised beds on each side. On the lower level we laid out geometrical beds and paved paths radiating from our sundial, and made a rectangular lily pond beyond.

The design was inspired by a picture in Georgina Masson's book on Italian gardens. When it was finished it looked very severe and also curiously lopsided. The informal planting of low shrubs and perennials took care of the severity after a few years and to correct the lopsidedness we designed and

39 Evening light: a lemon-yellow tree lupin dominates the yellow border beside the house

40 Pale daffodils carpet the ground beneath the fallen turkey oak, Quercus cerris

built a queer little building with a pointed roof. This is a dovecote and below the pigeons' storey we have decorated a small room with shells.

The east side of the house was treated quite differently. We took in part of the field, levelled a large space, built a ha-ha, pegged out three irregular island beds and sowed the lawn. Along the wall which divides this side of the garden from the formal part is an irregular planting of trees and shrubs and some herbaceous plants of the kind I like to think of as 'maquis' plants. For instance, there are cistuses, helichrysums, *Teucrium fruticans*, brooms and heaths. It is rather a jungle but I am afraid I am a fairly untidy gardener and would rather have profusion than neatness.

This was the way we started and since then we have pushed on into the wood on the northern slope at the back of the house and planted rhododendrons, camellias, magnolias and the like in rough grass round an open levelled space which was originally a bowling green. At the far end of this we built a tiny water garden with a waterfall made of granite gate posts. The water flows over these into a stone trough and is pumped up again, leaking on its way down over the primulas, irises, astilbes, kingcups and other thirsty plants.

The derelict walled garden has become a white garden. I wonder how many white gardens have been inspired by Sissinghurst? Here we made a great mistake that sadly cannot be rectified without spoiling the design. One imagines the perfect moment in a white garden will be at the end of a hot summer's day. You sit and gaze at the cool colours as the shadows begin to lengthen. However, we were stupid enough to put a nice stone bench facing towards the west. The result is that, at the imagined moment, the sun shines straight in your eyes. Sometimes I take a folding chair and go and sit at the opposite end!

I have a passion for walls, particularly when built of grey stone. We were lucky to find a good many here but nevertheless a few years back we made another walled garden. This time we decided against grass and paved it, leaving a large rectangular space in the middle and wide beds round the sides. Before I describe what we planted in this new plot, I must mention here that the great and famous Cornish gardens, several of which we now know well, are mostly given over to spring flowering shrubs and trees. After the end of June, there is little to see. One might think their owners all went abroad for the latter part of the year. Actually I believe the disease I call 'rhododendronitis' had so infected their creators that they did not think anything other than the tenderer Asiatic shrubs were worth growing. We were determined to have something to look at in July and August and later as well.

In the new walled garden I therefore imagined a place, isolated from the rest of the garden, where on an overcast day in high summer the warm and cheerful colours would raise our spirits. So we planned and planted it with shrubs and perennial plants whose flowers were in shades of red, orange and yellow; blues, pinks and mauves were banned. In order to cool things down a bit we put in all the red-leaved plants we could find and added some silvers as long as their flowers were not of the wrong colour. It was ironical that the next two summers turned out to be the hottest and driest that we have known down here. However, the summer of 1977 was back to normal.

As you may have realized the garden here is not small, although not on the scale of Edwardian splendours. I feel that as far as planning new areas is concerned, we have now bitten off every bit as much as we can chew. So this new garden is likely to be our last ambitious effort.

Some of the lovelist sights in the garden owe very little to our contrivance. In front of the house a large turkey oak was blown down about fifty years ago. It was only half uprooted and since then has struggled to twist its branches upwards. Arthur Rackham would have loved it. Underneath, some pale daffodils had naturalized themselves. To these we added snowdrops and planted crocuses round its skirts. I wish you could see it on a sunny morning in early March.

There is another completely unplanned picture which gives me enormous pleasure every year. In very early gardening days we cleared out the remains of a shrubbery in a corner of the spinney. We were starting to plant in the wood and wanted to blot out an unattractive shed. So we dumped down a small yew and an ungainly old *Philadelphus* a few feet in front of the shed. Now each July the white flowers of the *Philadelphus* pour out of the yew tree. It is a disgraceful old unpruned plant but I could not bear to have it touched.

June is a month that takes care of itself wrote Margery Fish, who through her writings and gifts to us in early gardening days, introduced me to so many good plants. In common with others at that time

41 Primula japonica *and other plants in the woodland garden*

42 *A floriferous lilac of the* Syringa x persica *group in May*

43 Leptospermum 'Red Damask' *in the south courtyard*

44 The woodland garden. The sun filters through, lighting the Queen Anne's lace

45 The new walled garden, with perennials and shrubs of red, orange and yellow

of year we have most of the ingredients of Tennyson's *Summer Night*. We have petals both crimson and white, a real Italian cypress, even a milk white peacock, not to mention several fonts.

I must now pay tribute to two people who have had a great influence on the course of gardening here. They are both named Alan. The first is my husband and the second our head gardener. My husband knows less about plants than I do but he has a better eye in planning large areas and bold effects. He is also quite unashamed in liking a riot of colour. He tells me that I only really like leaves and niminy-piminy plants, the ones I think of as little treasures. I enjoy unexpected corners, and, as I flatter myself, subtle plant combinations. One of my favourite plant associations is a patch of primrose violas in front of *Veronica gentianoides* and I dote on double primroses. Large yellow trumpet daffodils are not what I admire but I love the *triandrus* and *cyclamineus* hybrids. However, as all happily married people know, life is one long compromise, so sometimes he has his way and sometimes I get mine.

Alan Bryant took over the garden here about six years ago straight from his training at the Royal Horticultural Society's garden at Wisley, he was then twenty-four years old. Since Alan came, full of knowledge, energy and enthusiasm, we have started selling plants, for our propagation has increased a hundredfold.

My greatest pleasure in gardening is anticipation; to look at the green shoots and swelling buds and imagine what is to come. Even today as I write in late November, the snowflakes are pushing through and the camellias are covered in bud. We are ordering seeds and planting shrubs for next year. We are dividing, re-arranging, potting up and potting on. In spite of bitter experience and heart-rending losses, I always believe that next year is going to be the best. All pests and diseases will disappear effortlessly and somebody will invent a weedkiller with a built in computer, programmed to kill weeds and do no harm to one's treasures. You have to be an optimist or else give up your garden.

Patricia Boyd

Deene Park, Corby, Northamptonshire

The Hon. Mrs Brudenell's Garden

I MUST confess to being a planner and an 'enjoyer' but not a 'doer' in the garden. For me it is a place of enchantment where I find constant delight from wandering either alone, or with friends or strangers. Consequently I am still shamefully ignorant and it seems presumptuous even to mention my opinions or likes and dislikes. However, the two things that I regard as being of supreme importance are contrast and scale. The impact of symmetry, tidiness, form and space is enormously enhanced by the contrast of their opposites. If one moves through light to shade, from wide expanses to secluded corners where the focus can shrink myopically to enjoy some little detail, it adds a touch of mysterious magic. It can be boring walking round gardens where everything is the same size, and only looking downwards, where there is nothing to tempt the eye upwards such as a *Polygonum* frothing dizzily through an old oak or the rose, 'Rambling Rector', falling about with abandon through a yew. Contrasts of colour should I think be handled with tact, they must harmonize not clash with each other.

46 *Looking towards Deene Park across a canal that was extended in the 18th century to divide the garden from the park*

I think it is also vital to avoid bittiness. One or two little plants trying to fill too large a space look miserably mean. A feeling of abundance should prevail in any garden, large or small. It is a great advantage to have fine trees and water; they both add so much to the quality of light, particularly in the evening when the whole character of a garden is transformed. Then the shadows lengthen, the colours soften as the sun sinks lower, the scents become stronger, the waterfalls seem noisier and sometimes the whole lake turns an astonishing pink, reflecting the sunset.

Maybe one day I shall become a real gardener, but at the moment I am just grateful for the pleasure I get from our own and other people's gardens.

Marian Brudenell

47 A view from the grass walk that runs beside the long border – a principal feature of the garden. Statues of the four seasons mark the corners of a low wall round a grass bay, which leads to steps down to the canal

White Barn House

Elmstead Market

Essex

Mrs Andrew Chatto's Garden

GENERALLY SPEAKING, I would say that East Anglia is not famous for great gardens. There are notable exceptions of course, but glancing through most books on well-known gardens, luxuriously illustrated with enticing views and colourful close-ups, one rarely finds an East Anglian setting. There is probably one over-riding reason for this – our regional climate. We are in the driest part of the country, the rain-bearing winds from the west having shed most of their load by the time they arrive. Add to this a persistence of cold drying winds from the north-east, which blow all spring and half the summer, and gardening can be too disheartening altogether. The average yearly rainfall is about twenty-two inches, sometimes as little as fourteen inches. This, combined with wind and above average sunshine, makes drought an annual event, not an occasional hazard.

When I married I inherited a garden about seven miles from here where we struggled for seventeen years with both climate and soil conditions, having an impoverished chalky boulder clay. Through trial and error I learnt which plants would thrive and lost many which I should not have tried. Then, unexpectedly we decided to build a house on my husband's fruit farm, so we had the opportunity to create a new garden.

The site we chose was an overgrown shallow valley of two or three acres, slipped between our farm and our neighbours. Uncultivated and neglected it contained a few fine oaks and hollies towering above a confused tangle of blackthorn, bramble and bracken, with alder and willow along the deep spring-fed ditch which ran down the centre. The sun-facing slopes consisted of coarse gravel and fine sand. The opposite slope was made of a black water-retaining acid silt, while the lowest levels were wet clay. Here were widely varying conditions offering homes for a far greater range of plants than we had been able to grow before.

48 A view from the sitting-room window at White Barn House. Here Beth Chatto started her new garden with a lily pond, planting Cupressus arizonica, Juniperus communis *and other foliage plants*

47

49 (Left) Zantedeschia aethiopica 'Green Goddess' growing in a pond. 50 (Centre) Euphorbia myrsinites *in full flower*. 51 (Right) *The winter stems of* Rubus cockburnianus *woven as a birdcage*

My husband's life-long interest has been the natural association of plants, and in particular many of our garden plants. From his studies I have learnt that plants grow better and look better if planted as nearly as possible in the kind of conditions to which they have been adapted. Simplified, it is a matter of common sense not to plant shade-lovers and sun-lovers together. These factors led us to make three contrasting areas of garden. Around the low split-level house lying on the sun-baked gravel slopes we made our 'Mediterranean' garden, using aromatic plants like rosemary, *Cistus*, *Santolina* and *Artemisia* which would endure the cruel droughts. On the cooler slopes, with additional planting of trees and shrubs for shade, we envisaged lush foliage plants like hostas, adapted to woodland conditions, while the spring-fed ditch, in time was to become a series of watergardens.

A bulldozer crashed through the tanglewood and soon made a series of platforms for the house and terraces which eventually we made around it. The worthwhile trees were preserved, the rest swept away. A grab-line working on the farm reservoir just below the garden came in and the driver gouged out a small hole in the ditch bed and called it my lily pond. I planted a pampas grass on the bank which overhung it, and turned my mind to more pressing problems.

Much of the stock ferried over from our original garden was rowed out waiting for a home in the seemingly vast, empty landscape. We began with the garden around the house. We made the paths and terraces ourselves, either of paving, cobbles or gravel, knowing that grass would always be poor and parched in times of drought. For height we planted *Cupressus arizonica*, *Juniperus communis*, *Genista aetnensis* now fifteen feet high and a fountain of perfumed gold in July, with *Spartium junceum* almost as big. Beneath them groups of *Cistus* and *Olearia* spp provide bulk and background for the soft clouds or mounds of silvery greys which now clothe the once bare gravel. Mat forming plants creep out over the paving, softening the hard edges. Throughout the year bulbs spring up among these foliage plants. The year starts with early crocuses, fritillaries, species tulips and irises with alliums carrying on throughout the summer, to join more crocuses, sternbergias and nerines which carry colour almost into the short days of winter.

It was two or three years before I went back to the lily pond and decided that what was wrong with it was that it was too small and out of proportion with its surroundings. Over several years a set of five large pools has evolved separated by mown grass-covered dams and surrounded by a collection of

48

52 (Left) Digitalis parviflora. 53 Selinum tenuifolium *backed by the purple-leafed filbert.* 54 (Right) *A 'Gold Lace' type of primula*

moisture-loving trees, shrubs and plants. These pools are fed continually, regardless of drought, by springs which flow underground from the surrounding farmland.

Initially we had little help. The garden progressed slowly those first years. We had to have patience to create shelter from desiccating winds, and to grow up a background and framework to set off many of the plants which looked absurd in their loneliness. Three snowdrops are meaningless in empty space; they must be seen in drifts and patches, in the context of their companions. Much of my time was spent propagating new stock from seeds, berries and cuttings obtained from various seed lists and good gardening friends. Prominent among these was Sir Cedric Morris whose collection of plants and bulbs I would consider second to none. Certainly no one could be more generous, whether of plants, knowledge or ideas. I am greatly indebted to him.

We used very few weedkillers and then only on paths and drive-ways. Weeding was often a nightmare; beds became carpeted with annual meadow-grass and chickweed, chief offenders among dozens more natives who felt they had first right to be there.

About ten years ago I decided to start a small nursery. So began a new phase to my garden. With my two daughters away from home, it was also the beginning of a new life for me although I had no conception at the time of the extent to which my venture would grow.

Ten years later I am astonished how the nursery, like my plantings, has developed. I knew that flower arrangers were interested in unusual plants, as I would occasionally lecture to them and they, in turn, would visit the garden. Taking my plants to London for the first time was an event for us all and today I have six young local women whose development I enjoy watching as they learn to love the art and craft of growing plants, learn their names and characteristics, and how to care for them.

Having help is splendid, but, from the beginning, it made it necessary for me to think harder and deeper. I began to question the necessity for weeding the same patches repeatedly throughout the year. I relished those areas that were made trouble free by dense coverings of plants. If I could cut down the time spent on weeding, not only would there be more time to propagate plants, but perhaps we could make another pond, create a new shade garden, or plant a new entrance garden.

Thus I was led both to be more ambitious in extending the garden, and at the same time learning to plant with weed control foremost in my mind.

49

I made a second entrance border, backed by *Cupressus* and deciduous trees with drought-loving shrubs and cover plants used in much bolder groups. The soil has not been left bare since planting, the ground beneath the trees and shrubs being mulched annually with a thick layer of straw which has browned and flattened by spring. The front edge is almost covered now with *Stachys byzantinus*, *Saponaria ocymoides*, *Achillea* 'Moonshine' and several kinds of *Bergenia* which, on the poor gravel soil and in full sun, assume glorious tints of rose, carmine and bronzy-red in winter. Any open spaces are covered with a two inch layer of pulverized bark which stifles tiny weed seedlings as they try to struggle to the surface. Deep-rooted intruders like bindweed, thistle, nettle or dandelion are touched with a paintbrush loaded with a systemic weedkiller in June.

I still feel very hesitant about using weedkillers among plants, but with my garden and nursery still extending I have begun experimenting with a pre-emergence weedkiller called lenacil. Not all established plants tolerate it, but many do. Where we have not enough mulch to cover a bed entirely we use the crushed bark around those plants which would be adversely affected, and, after thoroughly cleaning and weeding we immediately spray all the bare soil. The effect, lasting about eight weeks, is quite miraculous as no germinating seedlings can emerge. My aim is that eventually the planting will itself cover the soil, but until that happens a combination of mulches and weedkillers help me to maintain large and complicated borders with, on average, barely one working day a week being spent in the garden, throughout the year, apart from grass maintenance.

When we made the original 'Mediterranean' garden we had all too little humus to incorporate into the raw soil. Added to this certain crocuses and pestilential species of alliums seeded into thyme mats, and generally things became out of hand. I decided to remove and preserve the smaller plants worth keeping, retaining the back-bone of trees and shrubs. Then we removed the top spit, bulbs and all. This was carted away with the still valued tractor, and spread around in a newly developing area where I hope to have troublesome but desirable bulbs naturalized around shrubs. Then, to increase the soil depth over almost pure gravel, we built a low retaining wall one concrete block high and

55 and 56 The dry garden. Paths have been made of gravel where grass would always have been poor. (Left) Genista aetnensis. (Right) Euphorbia species *and* Heracleum giganteum *set in a cobbled courtyard*

57 and 58 Two of the pools. Over several years a group of five large pools has evolved. They are separated by mown, grass-covered dams and surrounded by a collection of moisture-loving trees, shrubs and plants

infilled with good top soil, muck and peat well mixed. It sounds over-nutritious for drought-loving plants, but recent droughts have provoked me, and I had already made such a bed, with an inch or two of gravel grit for a mulch, along a hot south-west facing wall, raised about two feet, and the resulting growth is a joy. Everyday it is a pleasure to walk along it, and I revel in the contrasting forms, colours and textures of foliage, even in mid-winter. Over all the garden my policy is to incorporate garden compost or well-rotted muck whenever I want to renew a patch, to maintain and improve the humus content of the soil.

Although I am describing a garden which could be considered large by average standards today, having spread now over about four acres, there are small areas which are complete in themselves, and could be borrowed as ideas for planting in smaller gardens.

I am grateful for good books. Almost every book new to me provides some novel idea or approach, but those of Gertrude Jekyll, William Robinson, Margery Fish, Graham S. Thomas and Christopher Lloyd fall most easily out of my bookshelves and have contributed much to the designs in my garden.

Throughout the weeks, especially in summer, visitors come to enjoy the garden. I enjoy my visitors. But, on Sundays there is a blessed peace, to think, to plan, and to plant, alone. I need that too.

I am trying to make a garden that is of interest throughout the year, where no place need be shunned because of neglect. Every piece of soil is precious, and can provide a home for some plant, shrub or tree. I have no favourite place in my garden.

Beth Chatto

51

Broadleas, Devizes, Wiltshire

The Lady Anne Cowdray's Garden

IN 1946 I bought Broadleas, an early nineteenth-century house with attractive Regency features and a garden on greensand, an unknown quantity to me then. The garden had been totally neglected since 1939, and the dell was just a jungle of *Rhododendron ponticum* and bamboos. The ponticums were in flower when I first looked it over so I realized the soil could grow ericaceous plants. In retrospect the task I took on was daunting, but at the time I was shielded by inexperience.

At first I was too busy coping with a growing family to do much in the garden, but found time to plant a few basic trees, magnolias, beech and ash, and varieties of *Sorbus*. I inherited several large trees including a beautiful *Sequoia sempervirens* raised from the first importation nearly one hundred years ago. Now, after a further thirty years the dell has a good selection of unusual trees and shrubs, as greensand offers a home to all kinds. It is roughly four acres in extent and must have been an old river course, with steep banks on either side broadening out towards the bottom. The river now runs twenty feet underground and is my sole water supply. As an antidote to its high alkaline content I have innumerable tanks to catch rainwater.

The plants are perhaps too close together as with the steep banks the overhead canopy tends to be dense, but I cannot resist collecting beautiful and unusual specimens and magnolias are my great love. I am now planting *Nothofagus* spp, as yet little known, but with great potential as replacements for our dying elms and beech.

It took me several years to discover what was destroying so many of my best trees and shrubs. It was honey fungus and I have now read everything I can about it and tried every suggested remedy. There is no certain cure but I believe that 'Armillatox' can save a plant, if not too far gone, but you must be patient and wait two years for signs of recovery. The preventative I have used for the last three years is copper carbonate. We mix a large spoonful of this in the soil of all newly planted

59 *A circular* claire voyée *in a brick wall gives a view into the rose garden at Broadleas (plate 60). In the foreground are senecio and santolina*

60 *The sunken rose garden. Alpine strawberries seed themselves here between the paving stones and among the roses.* (Right) 61 *Early spring in the dell*

woody plants and I always remove every bit of fungus and dead wood. This treatment has so far proved effective. The main thing is to keep everything healthy as a plant under stress is the most likely to be attacked. Plants on the steep banks of the dell are very apt to dry out in the summer on this greensand, so I bank my beds with creosote-impregnated planks or peat blocks to level and hold the vital compost with which I try to feed every plant each year.

The house stands at the top of the dell surrounded by lawns on three sides. On the fourth a sunken rose garden is almost an extension of the house as it is enclosed by walls, one of which has an intriguing circular aperture to give a view-point in and out. Here I let alpine strawberries seed themselves between the paving stones and among the roses.

Roses look good against the grey Bath stone and I have chosen 'Mme Grégoire Staechelin', 'Mrs. Sam McGredy' and 'Shot Silk' to clothe the south front of the house. Among them are two wisterias, one a magnificent *W. floribunda* 'Macrobotrys syn. multijuga' with racemes well over a yard long, the other was bought as white *venusta*, but when it flowered it turned out mauve.

To carry out my ambition of having at least one plant in flower all the year round I have a winter garden with *Rhododendron nobleanum*, *Schisostylis*, and various mahonias, hebes and salvias. Under a large beech tree a bed of cyclamen species continue in flower for months. I love them so much that I have planted them round several other trees to give a splash of colour in October.

To take care of my more tender plants I built a curved wall facing south, with polythene protection projecting two feet from the top, and in winter Rokolene netting is hung down in front. Three fragrant shrubs, *Wattakaka sinensis*, *Rhododendron* 'Lady Alice Fitzwilliam', and *Trachelospermum jasminoides* are among others that flower and seem quite happy.

I have a secret garden enclosed by a wall and hedges of *Prunus × blireana*. I had never seen it grown as a hedge before but longed to try, and I am so glad that I did as it has been most successful, attractive all the year round with its double pink flowers in spring and coppery-wine foliage for nine months of

53

the year. Here there are only small trees and shrubs, acers, two eucalyptus kept low, *Hibiscus*, *Abutilon* × 'Suntense' and *Hydrangea paniculata* 'Tardina' which was a present from the Savill Gardens. The hedges give such good shelter that even *Melianthus major* survives. Salvias are a vast family, mostly from hot climes, but I am trying out every one I can get hold of.

62 *A spring corner: cyclamen, snowdrops and crocuses*   63 *A fine* Magnolia sargentiana

I have not mentioned shrub roses, a serious omission, as although they came into my life rather late, they now occupy a great part of my heart, and to my surprise, I find I have sixty-six different kinds, plus a few Floribundas. Most are in a mixed hedge alongside the entrance drive. 'Roseraie de l'Hay' is my favourite rugosa with the hybrid 'Sarah Van Fleet' a close second. 'Marguerite Hilling' flowers almost perpetually and is my favourite 'modern shrub', and 'Mme Grégoire Staechelin' my favourite climber. Perhaps next year others may take precedence as young plants get bigger and better.

My interest in gardening began at an early age with miniature plants in stone troughs. During the war I was able to enlarge my horizons and start a woodland garden in Scotland while running my husband's house as a hospital. However, my real interest in gardening did not develop until I came here, and has since been fostered by many talented and knowledgeable gardening friends. One I must mention is the late Captain Jenkinson, a friend for forty years and, at one time, owner of Knapp Hill Nurseries. He had a phenomenal memory and love of plants. He often came here and gave me advice but complained that I never took it! Not entirely true, I may add. I have listened and learned from friends, and from visits to gardens here and abroad, often in company with the International Dendrology Society and International Camellia Society. Both have members with a huge cache of knowledge and taste, to whom I am grateful for imparting so much of it to amateurs like me.

12A Selwood Place
London SW7

Mrs Anthony Crossley's Garden

THE ORIGINAL house was built in 1821 and behind it I found a big L-shaped garden, one hundred and eleven feet long, leading off eighty feet to the right in an expanse of grass and island beds. This was Mr. Selwood's eighteenth-century nursery garden in Salad Lane. When I saw all that land I wanted to dance for joy. You must be ready for your luck, so I went straight ahead and designed the house and garden until four o'clock in the morning when I fell asleep, exhausted but determined to live there.

Then on to the scene as a friend of friends came Russell Page, one of our greatest garden designers. I had read his book *The Education of a Gardener* with intense attention. I knew that he would have a wonderful idea surpassing any of my own and after two minutes he said: 'Have your narrow bed in the sun on the right, and your wide bed in the shade under the high wall on the left.' He drew me a charming plan of the whole garden and terrace, nearly all of which has been carried out. I have always had the French feeling for form, with wildness within that form, to be seen from a drawing-room window, with an architectural shape, in this case my summerhouse, at the end of the vista.

It is impossible to garden and keep an agitated mind. Working in the garden gives health and sleep.

Clare Crossley

64 and 65 *The garden at Selwood Place as seen from the sitting-room window.* (Below) *Rose* 'Alberic Barbier' *cascades down the left side of the garden.* (Right) *Large bushes of* Artemisia arborescens *show off the pink rose,* 'Zephirine Drouhin'

The Countess of Haddington's Garden

THE LANDS of Tyninghame stand within sight and sound of the sea, its history stretching back into antiquity, romantic and obscure.

It is known that in 941 the Vikings stormed through East Lothian followed by the Danes and Normans, who in turn created further havoc. It was the Danes who burned the village and church of Tyninghame founded three centuries before by the pious St. Baldred of the Bass.

It is next mentioned in the earliest known Scottish Charter extant, that of King Duncan dated 1094, when the King gave Tyninghame in alms to the monks of St. Cuthbert and it became monastic.

For the following three centuries it was owned by the See of St. Andrews. It can be conjectured that during the next three hundred years the monks must assuredly have made some sort of garden and possibly grown herbs, apple trees and vegetables, but of this there is no trace.

Today one of the few visible reminders of this past is the lovely little *Tulipa sylvestris* growing in a small coppice by the river on the site of what was once a Roman village. It is supposed to have been brought over by the Romans when they settled in these parts. The ruin of the Norman church remains too, with its dog tooth arches catching the evening sun, creating a feeling of deep peace.

66 *The herbaceous border at Tyninghame. Pink, mauve and white roses cover the old walls, while clumps of cotton lavender are massed in the foreground*

67 The secret garden, which is Lady Haddington's favourite part of her large garden. Here the beds are filled with old roses in subdued colours.
Right. 68 Arched supports for climbing roses and ornamental vines span a path edged with nepeta, dianthus, campanula and other old-fashioned flowers

In 1628, the first Earl of Haddington purchased the property and thus Tyninghame became the permanent home of the Haddington family. Since then, each generation has carried on the loving task of improving the land and planting the woods.

But it was Thomas, the sixth Earl, a pioneer of farming and foresty in Scotland who, assisted and encouraged by his wife Helen Hope, initially planned and laid out the extensive Tyninghame woodlands. The Earl, in a letter to his grandson which takes the form of, 'A Treatise on the manner of raising Forest Trees', describes his first coming to Tyninghame in 1700 and finding 'not above 14 acres set with trees and gardens surrounding the house'.

We are located on a very exposed part of the east coast of Scotland, which makes it difficult sometimes to establish newly planted shrubs and trees. To aggravate the situation, the soil here is very sandy in places, and therefore porous and the small rainfall of twenty-one inches per annum soon percolates away. Invariably, in April and May we are subjected to dry and searing easterly winds, sometimes of weeks' duration. The water table drops dramatically, leaving the newly planted trees and shrubs with their roots in dry soil, and us with a high casualty list. Broad leaved species are subjected to very late frosts, sometimes well into May, one particular frost being noted as late as 6 June (1962). Should we be fortunate enough to get a wet April and May, the picture is quite different, as losses are then negligible. After a year or two, when the root systems get down to the moister soil, growth is rapid.

We came here to spend the summer months for the first time in 1952 and then for longer spells. From the beginning the garden beckoned to me as I looked through the windows from the house, and it was not long before spades and forks were busy and further plans materialized. It was a delight to find in the walled garden peach houses and glorious Muscat grape houses. The grapes were carefully packed every year to make the long journey for exhibition at the Southport Show. Usually the head gardener came back with the second prize which he assured us should have been the first, if a rival exhibitor had not stolen into the building at the dead of night and rubbed the bloom off the Tyninghame grapes! However, we were well satisfied with second prize.

As I have already mentioned, the soil here is very light and consists of sand, a little peat and loam. Rainfall being so low, it is necessary to enrich the soil by adding leaf mould, peat and hops, with a dash of manure. Our climate is quite temperate apart from the occasional storms coming in off the sea, and everything grows with great exuberance. Nevertheless, my hopes can be dashed after a cold spell when a plant which I have cherished for four or five years suddenly collapses. Last year, just such a treasure, *Clianthus puniceus* was completely destroyed in the severe frost, with not even a faint sign of life remaining at its base.

I have always loved flowers and gardens, perhaps because my earliest recollection is associated with our home which stood on the banks of the swift flowing River St. Lawrence in Canada and contained a delightful vegetable and flower garden. Thanks to our gardener, who came from 'the old country', we were each encouraged to have a tiny plot in which to grow our favourite annuals such as mignonette, nasturtiums, herbs and other old fashioned flowers. But it was my mother who first lit the flame in our hearts by her original approach of giving each child the task, once a week, of picking and helping to arrange a vase of flowers in the house, thus creating an interest and personal involvement in the garden. To this day, when passing a lilac tree and catching its exquisite scent, memories of those happy childhood days return. The gardens here contain a large number of the various mauve and white lilacs, and a few of the outstanding ones that do well are the 'Maud Nottcutt' variety and 'Vestale', both white, as well as 'Buffon', a soft pink and 'Esther Staley'. I like to think that it is a rather common failing to plant one's favourites too close together. If this is so, I must confess to being the worst offender for after some years' growth, I find the branches of the lilacs stretching across beds of roses and almost suffocating their bloom. This entails double the amount of labour, having to cut away lower branches to bring in light and air or lifting the roses to an open position.

The terraces occupy a fair expanse of the layout around the house and contain a parterre and borders on two levels. Traditionally, these were planted with annuals, and my first task was to alter the planting to save our very reduced help. In these formal beds by the house, we now have yellow roses, chiefly the Hybrid Tea 'King's Ransom' and 'Iceberg' (Floribunda). In the centre of each bed the climbing rose 'Golden Showers' climbs up a wooden support and in the white rose beds standard

'Icebergs' complete the scheme. For the rest of the garden, including the terraces, the planting of which I altered considerably, the colours have always been kept very subdued, with mauves, pinks, yellows, whites and occasionally a very deep red or yellow to light up a corner, as the overall design.

In the wide herbaceous borders I planted shrubs and small trees using the colourful *Acer palmatum* for colour effect and the weeping pear *Pyrus salicifolia* 'Pendula'. I have found that the different grey shrubs such as *Senecio* 'Sunshine', *Cineraria maritima*, tree paeonies and groups of lavender

69 *The terrace by the house. These formal beds are planted with 'Golden Shower' roses on wooden supports, standard 'Icebergs' and Hybrid Tea 'King's Ransom'*

70 *The old walled vegetable garden. This is now dominated by a wide grass walk with clipped yew hedges and stone statues. In the far distance are the Lammermuir hills*

make a foil to the pink stone of the house. On the lower terrace, I have planted against the wall *Carpenteria californica*, clumps of *Cotinus obovatus*, shrub roses, grey foliage plants of all kinds and at intervening spaces there are arbours which contain climbing roses, *Lonicera* and *Clematis*. Two centre basins occupy equi-distant spaces on this terrace and in these I planted 'Hidcote' lavender with *Clematis montana* growing on a support in the centre and at each corner the shrub *Cotinus coggygria purpureus*. This latter, with its deep crimson colour, proved to be ornamental, but it was one of my big mistakes. It has taken over most of the space in these stone basins and is now forcing its way between the small cracks in the stone.

Perhaps my favourite part of the garden started out as a rough bit of ground that verged onto the parterre by the house. I had waited some time studying what seemed a forgotten area, roughly an acre of long grass. It appeared to cry out for someone's attention. To plant and enhance the appearance of the other parts of the garden, reducing the labour at the same time, had proved a satisfying and fascinating experience, but this was a different sort of challenge and one not to be resisted. It was the creation of a small garden in which I could work happily alone without having to call in too much help. It was also my intention to grow old fashioned roses and other favourite plants. I studied many layouts and finally found my inspiration in Rapin's poem 'Of Gardens' and in John James' translation

59

71 The knot garden: box edging infilled with lavender

72 Philadelphus 'Avalanche' of the Lemoinei group

of *The Theory and Practice of Gardening*, an eighteenth-century French book with garden designs, adapting a drawing to my own more simple taste.

With the help of our highly capable gardener we started the long and tedious job of measuring to get the right size for each bed, then placing the thin ropes into the shapes and finally we started the digging. It was not long before we found there was an underlay of every kind of rubbish, including broken china, glass and metal. In fact it turned out to be the base of a long disused Victorian tennis court. Undefeated we battled on, and now it has been christened 'The Secret Garden'.

The beds are filled with old roses with such romantic names as 'Reine des Violettes', 'Ispahan', 'Commandant Beaurepaire', 'Honorine de Brabant', the lovely hybrid musk 'Felicia', 'Comte de Chambord', the white 'Madame Hardy' and many more. In the middle bed our estate joiner built an arbour containing a stone figure representing summer. The surrounding beds contain arched supports for climbing roses and one of my favourite honeysuckles, *Lonicera × americana*. There are lilies and *Agapanthus*, centaureas, *Stachys* 'Silver Carpet', *Helichrysum splendidum*, *Santolina* and *Senecio*. The grey leafed plants seem to form a perfect foil of soft colours which melt into the overall effect.

For me this garden, a corner of Tyninghame, is a miniature paradise. It is by no means perfect, but it has come to be an oasis of rest and quiet, where visitors can wander at ease and where each winding path can bring a fresh surprise. This is surely something of value in our turbulent world.

Sarah Haddington

Lady Heald's Garden

THE GREAT and wonderful thing about a garden is that it is yours to mould in the way you wish. If you are lucky enough, as I have been to inherit a garden created over the last two hundred and fifty years, you cannot re-design it but you can cherish and renew it.

The garden as a whole is on three different levels and was originally designed in about 1728 by Sarah, Duchess of Marlborough after she had left Blenheim. Trees provide the frame into which the picture goes. I know it is said about planting trees that one is doing it for the next generation, but I have had the satisfaction of planting a tulip tree thirty years ago which has been flowering for eight years, so has a *Catalpa* planted for the Coronation in 1952. I have a very strong feeling that where plants seed themselves one should let them grow. Naturally I take cuttings of various plants, and I am especially thrilled when a cutting from a rather rare species takes.

73 *A corner of the garden at Chilworth Manor in spring. The garden was designed by Sarah, Duchess of Marlborough in about 1728*

My garden is certainly not a large and stately one. On the other hand it is not particularly small and there is only one gardener and my husband and me with some weekly 'maintenance' to cope with it all. But gardeners or no gardeners, to me it is still well worth battling on because through it I can always find peace and refreshment for myself and I find too, I can give pleasure to a great many people.

Daphne Heald

74 *Part of the original walls. The walls enclose the three-tier terraced garden, and today are covered with varieties of the older roses including 'Ophelia' and an unnamed, extremely old shrub rose*

75 *The Duchess's steps are part of the original design. This terrace makes a splendid setting for a pair of spectacular Senecio 'Sunshine'. Fine trees, including some ancient apples, provide a framework for the whole garden*

Hadspen House, Castle Cary, Somerset

Mrs Paul Hobhouse's Garden

I SHOULD wish my ideal garden to assume the functions of a sculpture gallery, with plants as well as statues and stonework contributing architectural shape and form. At the same time the whole or each part of the garden should have the characteristics of a landscape painting with a strong sense of composition, attained by skilful use of harmony and contrast between shapes of plants, and between colours and textures of leaves and flowers. Each plant can enhance its neighbour, and each group of plants can contribute to the visual effect of a particular section. The separate and defined areas within the whole must be held together by planting schemes which entice the visitor on. Finally, the perfect garden should stimulate by the inclusion of plants which are of interest, making a sort of horticultural encyclopaedia *in vivo*; plants which inform as well as please. I hope that at Hadspen we have incorporated some of these features.

When we came here in 1968, we found an eight-acre garden in which little had been done for thirty years. On an earlier eighteenth-century plan, with high south-facing walls, an east-facing sloping kitchen section and some mature trees, my husband's grandmother had carved out a terraced area near the house, built walls, steps, and a fountain, and added several magnificent trees. Three Scots pines dominate a woodland slope, and a line of old yew trees follow the contours parallel to the walls above, to help contain a micro-climate for tender plants. A tulip tree, a copper beech, and a dilapidated horse chestnut make focal points and dictate the pattern of replanning.

The garden is on a south-facing slope to the east of the house. Frost drains away into the fields beyond, but because of the angle of slope, drought can cause serious problems. The soil has a pH ratio of about 6.8 so true calcifuge plants such as rhododendrons and most of the *Ericaceae*

76 *A paved path at Hadspen. Time-consuming edging of grass paths has been eliminated everywhere*

will not thrive, but shallow rooted plants on the borderline of lime tolerance seem to grow well.

The garden divides itself into three distinct styles or themes but throughout them all I have used plants in very similar ways. I have to consider carefully how best to save labour as, apart from mowing, I take the place of the six gardeners who worked here in the early 1900s. Now that I have got rid of the perennial weeds by using chemicals, mulches and black polythene, foliage plants either cover the ground, or make billowing shapes at a higher level to form the layer of underplanting for trees and shrubs above. In the wild or natural garden I use massed effects of shrubs which create a balanced pattern to fit the scale of the garden, while in the more formal areas I use flowing plant lines to break rigid patterns. Staccato leaves such as phormiums make excellent neighbours for the gentler shapes of rounded bushes, besides being useful as gateway plants, to frame a view or to lead on into another part of the garden. I have tried to eliminate all time-consuming edging tasks by using paving stone between the grass and soil of beds, or by using an air-cushion type of mower.

In the landscape garden section, I've planted curving island beds against a background of old dark yews. Here pale pittosporums, *Eucalyptus* and the startling foliage of a tree such as *Acer pseudo-platanus* 'Brilliantissimum' are underplanted with the old double daylily, the early spring foliage of which is almost pale gold. A weeping pear is set off by a massed and weed-suppressing bed of *Brunnera macrophylla*. The Scots pines, in a splendid group, dominate the woodland where I've used plants with contrasting greens as foliage, and lime-green, white and yellow flowers. In dark corners golden-leaved shrubs startle and surprise. Hellebores, especially the *orientalis* hybrids and cyclamen give brighter flowers, but not the hot colours more suitable for the formal areas in full sun.

In the midst of curving beds we have a meadow area, a strict rectangle, surrounded by mown lawn-paths, and flourishing with a diversity of spring and summer bulbs and perennials. We cut this wild area at the end of August and hope for a hot September to bake the bulbs while the grass is short.

From here a grass pathway leads on past bamboos, to another south-facing slope recently planted with trees for foliage, bark, and skeleton form as well as autumn colour. Longer grass, kept at three to four inches, forms beds to set off these trees, which make a satisfying contrast to the shorter grass paths which frame them. At the bottom of the slope, in the dampest part of the garden, I have new plantings of bamboos, rodgersias, astilbes and hostas with woodland shrubs which prefer moisture

77 and (centre) 78 The fountain garden. Luxuriant planting with groups of euphorbias, hostas and other foliage plants. (Right) 79 A rectangular water reservoir, edged with sun-loving plants

80 *The landscape garden. Curving island beds of golden shrubs flank the meadow area*

81 *The woodland garden under snow, dominated by three Scots pines*

and like shelter from the early morning sun. Huge species roses give colour and fragrance from the end of June to August, and many of these contribute beautiful hips and coloured foliage later in the season.

The second distinct area has a rectangular water reservoir, edged by sun-loving plants. Here, in a micro-climate created by another sheltered wall, I have indulged in pure planting ecstasies. Shrubs and climbers support and protect and intertwine, with little regard to design. A profusion of tropical looking leaves, mingled with the grey foliage of plants from hot and dry countries, gives interest and colour. I have used *Drimys winteri*, *Hoheria sexstylosa* and *Abutilon vitifolium* to give strong pyramidal shapes against the wall and tender plants support, protect and jostle each other.

The third area of the garden contains the walled kitchen garden and the old greenhouses, now adapted for propagation. In 1975 Eric Smith, the hellebore and hosta specialist, came from his nursery 'The Plantsmen', and we now run a small retail unit ourselves. We specialize in his perennials, which he continues to breed, and in the more interesting and rarer shrubs, particularly evergreens, my greatest interest, and now becoming difficult to obtain.

The walled garden has nursery beds round the edges, while down the centre of the garden I have made double borders, backed with beech hedges, almost entirely planted with Australasian shrubs. This is an experimental area, and I've shielded these tender plants from wind and early morning sun by planting cross hedges of *Griselinia littoralis* to form protective bays. In the lower garden the planting is more formal with another double border interplanted with hybrid Rugosa roses and clipped domes of *Phillyrea latifolia*. On a cross axis, a new planting of young espalier apples is set off by giant catmint. In one quarter shrub roses, grown in the nursery on their own roots, are planted formally. Varieties are chosen for value of shape, foliage, and fruit as well as flower. I hope this walled area now conveys a coherence of design, with horticultural interest and workmanlike utilitarianism rather different in concept from the purely ornamental.

In all planning and planting I have been constantly influenced by going to other gardens. Visiting

65

gardens of historic importance has led to some appreciation of the significance of trends in design, as well as teaching me how plants were used when first introduced. Reading garden history and early garden texts and manuals has stimulated me to experiment with old techniques appropriate to this garden. At the same time our own climatic situation has encouraged me to become interested in plants from specific countries.

One of the pleasures of having a retail nursery, with constant visitors, is the stimulation that is added to normal gardening life. I learn continually from listening to comments and the more expert send me hurrying to the reference books. Constructive ideas can lead to new thoughts and new meanings for the whole conception of the garden.

Penelope Hobhouse.

82 and 83 The south-facing sides of the house. Here several tender shrubs are nurtured, as well as a spectacular group of Euphorbia wulfenii

Used in the Meadow Area
Snakeshead fritillary (*Fritillaria meleagris*), Bee orchid (*Orchis apifera*), Spotted orchid (*Orchis maculata*), Cowslip (*Primula veris*), Cranesbill (*Geranium*), Moon daisies (*Chrysanthemum leucanthemum*), Velvet flower-de-luce (*Hermodactylus tuberosus*), Anemones.

Tender plants
Trachelospernum jasminoides, *Eriobotrya japonica,* *Nandina domestica,* *Callistemon,* *Leptospermum,* Olearias, *Rosa laevigata* 'Anemonoides', *Buddleia auriculata,* *Eupatorium ligustrinum.*

Pusey House, Faringdon, Oxfordshire

Mrs Michael Hornby's Garden

WE FOUND Pusey House and garden in 1935. The garden, a wilderness of great beauty with the unspoilt Georgian house standing proudly in the centre. Although the garden was neglected, it had wonderful trees, a small lake, walls, enclosed gardens, Victorian evergreen shrubberies, intersected with numerous paths and lawns. There were no flowers or flowering shrubs but endless possibilities.

We started with destruction: uprooting the Victoriana of laurel, box, yew and wellingtonias, grassing over paths, abolishing the formal rose garden and pulling out the vast box hedge, which concealed a ten foot Cotswold stone wall, later to become the backdrop to our huge herbaceous border. We had bonfires every weekend, with enthusiastic and willing helpers. Then we asked Geoffrey Jellicoe, that well-known garden architect whose work we had admired, to redesign the terrace and central steps. This he did with great success, and it is now the axis of the whole layout.

Then we endured five years of frustration through the war of 1939, during which we still made bonfires, a splendid occupation for friends in the services who happened to be around. When the war was over we started creating in earnest. We had had five years to think and plan. My imagination knew no bounds and my vision was packed with images of possibilities of colour, shape and vistas, as

84 The 'Chinese Chippendale' bridge over the lake at Pusey. Good use is made of the water's edge with hardy arums, primulas and bold groups of foliage plants

well as planning how to incorporate the legacy of trees, walls, lake-sides and open spaces. The pleasure garden covered an area of about fifteen acres which over the years we have reclaimed, planning on a large scale. Beds and planting had to be bold and clumps of whatever we planted had to contain many of one kind. Meanwhile, by ceaselessly visiting gardens old and new for pure pleasure, and by reading and talking to gardeners I unconsciously made gardening a great occupation and interest. I visit the R.H.S. shows, and many gardens and nurseries, everywhere.

I am very aware of colour and this garden could be called colour conscious. It has grown in size and stature, and now it is open to the public we have to be constantly on our toes to keep up the standard.

The visitor enters the garden through a double herbaceous border, flanking a grass path, planted in rainbow colours starting with reds through mauve, yellow, blue and white. This border ends with an ornamental gate leading to a vista of lawns, lake, woods and shrubberies. If possible I plant with no earth visible, so that weeds are suffocated and plants support each other thus minimizing staking. Trial and error is the best way to succeed with herbaceous borders, and it is easy to chop and change. They should not be planted flanking a grass path; a stone flag or gravel edge is much better. It is impossible to keep the grass tidy under floppy front liners such as helianthemums, *Dianthus*, or *Nepeta*.

The water garden came next. We've enjoyed and learnt from those in the Savill garden, planted with astilbes, *Iris siberica, Alchemilla mollis, Lobelia cardinalis, Lysimachia,* antholyzas and rodgersias galore. Arums and primulas are very hardy and increase from seed given real dampness, or submergence. When the lake rises in winter we have often skated over the arums which have been none the worse for it. To the water garden on higher ground we attached a shrubbery mainly red and grey, a successful combination, underplanted with aquilegias and foxgloves.

Still cutting our way into shrubberies, with the help and advice of Captain Bobbie Jenkinson and

85 *The terrace on the south side of the house. Brilliant helianthemums and other sun-loving plants grow generously through the paving*

86 *Lady Emily's garden. Four of the eight rose beds are filled with the reputedly disease-free Hybrid Tea rose 'Violinista costa'*

87 *Looking through the fine, wrought-iron gate towards the double herbaceous borders, which are planted in rainbow colours. The central grass path has a stone flag edging to protect the grass from floppy front-line plants*

Major Edward Compton of Newby Hall, we made ideal cubicles for tender material, opening entrances and exits and making paths. It is surprising how much wood you can cut out of mature trees to their improvement, and we now thin cherries, acers and sorbus, which we planted thirty years ago.

When designing a new bed I mark it out with a large quantity of bamboos or stakes and string, easily altered until you feel happy with curves, points and circles related to straight lines. The eye must never be uneasy. A garden hose is an excellent liner and it remains where you put it, is easily kicked into shape and is very visible. Another idea when making a new bed which you are not quite sure will fit into the landscape is to cut large bushy branches, approximately the mature height of your chosen plants, hedgerow growth is very suitable, and plonk them where you want your bed to be. You can then be sure if this is the right venture and either scrap it, alter it or carry on. I try not to have clumps of

88 The main herbaceous border. This is backed by a magnificent ten-foot-high Cotswold stone wall

89 Rosa filipes 'Kiftsgate' behind a statue of an 18th-century shepherd

spikes next to each other or too many neighbouring horizontals or cosy pouffes, attempting to interspace these. In a large area nine at least in any one clump is desirable.

The first of the many mistakes I made was attaching new beds to old shrubberies, instead of creating free standing ones. The dark green of the shrubs can be used for contrast, but the beds should be islands. I fell into this trap because I was trying to convince my husband that I was not making the garden any larger, just altering it a bit! Some of these attachments have been successful but not all. The last very successful bed is known as Michael's bed. It is almost free standing, in shades of green with euphorbias, hostas, *Angelica*, hellebores, asphodels, *Acanthus*, bupleurum, *Phytolacca americana*, *Arum italicum* and bergenias, with *Gunnera* on the lake side.

There are several other areas of the garden all quite different, and created one by one. A part we cheekily call Westonbirt, because of a few interesting flowering trees, has a bed attached, successfully this time, to an old wall of holly, box and thuja which is at its best in August and September. I won quite a battle about making the main shrubbery free standing. It is large and very successful but not particularly original except possibly for a bold clump of *Cotinus coggygria* 'Royal Purple' very similar to 'Notcutt's variety', thickly planted round with *Nerine bowdenii*. In the variegated beds, all silver and gold, the only other colour allowed is mauve.

Most charming of all is the little walled garden known as 'Lady Emily's garden'. Lady Emily Herbert married Philip Pusey in 1822. Philip Pusey was one of the founders of the Royal Agricultural Society and carried out many agricultural experiments at Pusey where he lived from 1828–55. In the little garden are eight beds where we try to have colour and scent for many months of the year. On the walls we have a fine *Magnolia × soulangiana* 'Alba Superba' and a *Hydrangea sargentiana*, with *Clematis* rambling through them and other host shrubs.

Our soil is alkaline, light, poor stuff which needs a lot of feeding, with leafmould, organic manures and fertilizers. But don't despair, when I started gardening I thought all that was necessary was a hole in the ground and firming. Oh! the losses that occurred. Now every tree, shrub or plant is lovingly planted with bone meal, leafmould, peat or whatever is necessary, the ground well dug in every direction, the flowers amply manured and the roses fed when planted and then regularly throughout the growing season. Opinions change but Mr Mattock recommends thiophanate-methyl for roses to deter mildew and blackspot, with a foliar feed added every alternate time. Weed killers here are an essential. Hoeing and digging as well as staking, pruning, grass cutting, tying in, propagating, and a vegetable garden could not be managed with a staff of three men and a couple of very part time O.A.P.s, over fifteen acres, without the help of paraquat. We also use weedkillers on the paths once a year and a number of others elsewhere. We propagate plants, which can be seen growing here, for sale in our small garden centre. We are always begging from, and exchanging with, other gardening friends.

I was given an excellent home-made garden note book, with an index which reads: Plants I have promised; Promises made to me; Stolen ideas; Wants; Successes; Failures; Hints for growing difficult plants; Seen at shows, nurseries, gardens; Work for next Spring, Summer, Autumn, Winter. At the end is a page or two for each corner of the garden so that notes on each can be made.

This account of our garden is by no means an exhaustive one, and if I were to rewrite it next year it would probably be different, as the beauty of gardening is that in striving for perfection one is always learning and changing. We could never have got where we have without good professional help and it is everything to have a head gardener who is an enthusiast and receptive to new ideas, and we have got such a man now in Ken Cotton. His predecessor was here for forty years and grew up in the garden. As long as there are men like these to pass on the torch to the younger generation, the great gardens of England will continue to flourish.

Nicole Hornby

PLANTS USED IN MY MIXED HERBACEOUS BORDER

Reds: Potentilla 'Gibson's Scarlet', Geraniums, *Phormium tenax* 'Purpureum', *Salvia grahamii*, Paeonies, *Phlox*, Roses, Dahlias, Antirrhinums.

Yellow: Euphorbia polychroma, Hypericums, *Potentilla arbuscula*, *Inula hookeri*, Golden Rod, Dahlias, *Bartonia aurea, Limnanthes.*

White and Grey: Phlox, *Buddleia fallowiana, Rosa* 'Iceberg', *Galtonia candicans, Cineraria maritima* 'White Diamond', *Romneya coulteri*, Cardoons, Onopordons, *Anaphalis*, Antirrhinums, *Nicotiana.*

Mauve: Phlox, *Sedum* 'Autumn Joy', *Penstemon* 'Unripe grapes', *Rosa* 'Lavender Lassie', *Erigeron, Salvia candelabrum, Salvia farinacea* 'Blue Spike', *Salvia* officinalis 'Purpurascens', Dahlias.

Blue: Agapanthus 'Headbourne hybrids', *Salvia ambigens*, Irises, Veronicas, *Hibiscus*, Buddleias, *Aster frikartii, Aster amellus* 'King George', *Echium* 'Blue Bedder'.

Variegated, Golden and Grey Leafed Plants: Brunnera macrophylla 'Variegata', *Iris foetidissima* 'Variegata,' *Philadelphus coronarius* 'Variegatus', *Weigela florida* 'Variegata', *Filipendula ulmaria* 'Aurea', *Philadelphus coronarius* 'Aureus', *Humulus lupulus* 'Aureus', *Cornus alternifolia* 'Argentea', *Buddleia* 'Lochinch'.

Used in variegated beds, with silver and gold: Cornus alternifolia 'Argentea', *Brunnera macrophylla* 'Variegata', *Iris foetidissima* 'Variegata', *Philadelphus coronarius* 'Aureus', *Filipendula ulmaria* 'Aurea', *Philadelphus coronarius* 'Variegatus', *Weigela florida* 'Variegata', *Humulus lupulus* 'Aureus', *Buddleia* 'Lochinch'.

Howick, Alnwick, Northumberland

The Lady Mary Howick's Garden

HOWICK LIES on the coast of Northumberland, a county famous for beautiful scenery, but not for gardens. This is not surprising, as it must be exposed to longer bouts of north and east winds than almost anywhere else in England. Fortunately, we have a micro-climate of our own, partly because we are close to the sea, and partly because of superb shelter. During the Napoleonic wars when the Tories were in office for thirty years the Whig landlords retired to their country estates and planted trees, and today, these are the main beauty of the place.

Altogether, the garden covers perhaps fifteen acres, most of which is on limestone, and it was only in 1930 that three or four acres of acid soil were found to exist on top of a whinstone outcrop quite close to the house. This discovery was very welcome to my father, who spent the rest of his life planting a woodland garden. It is this piece of woodland which I have made particularly my own. The soil is a very good loam throughout, and needs little addition in the way of feeding stuffs. Bracken is the best mulch, and helps to preserve moisture round the plants in dry seasons. Weed killer is only allowed on the main paths.

I am lucky in having my father's planting as the background against which to plan. Thirty-year-old rhododendrons, magnolias, eucryphias and acers are round every corner, all of them of wonderful quality. They were either grown from seed collected by the Asian expeditions of the '20s and '30s, or else obtained as plants from famous gardens such as Westonbirt, Wakehurst, or St. Nicholas. Those were the days when there was plenty of labour. Owner gardeners all seemed to know each other, and there was freemasonry of exchange, not only of plants, but also of ideas and enthusiasm.

90 Magnolia campbellii at Howick against a background of Scots pine and blue sky. A remarkable sight so far north

91 *A view of the house, looking across some of the fifteen acres of garden,
which enjoys a mild coastal climate. Many of the trees which today are such a
feature of the garden, were planted during the Napoleonic wars*

It is very hard, looking at the garden today, to say where I began to build upon these foundations. Gardens grow by themselves whether you want them to or not, and plants get too big for their neighbours and new dispositions have to be made. Also, over the last fifteen years trees have blown down, honey fungus has taken its toll, drought and snow have had to be coped with, and cold late springs full of east wind have been the very devil. These things are part of the experience of every gardener, and in themselves dictate change. More seriously, in my garden, the candelabra primulas have suddenly refused to flourish, and I think I miss them more than anything else. They were so lovely in their many-coloured profusion, and for ten years after I took over they were the main beauty of June and July. Then they started to die out, whether from disease or eelworm I do not know, and now they only do well where I can find new ground for them, which is not always easy. However, meconopsis of all kinds do extraordinarily well, and they have largely filled the gap left by the primulas.

I love blue flowers, especially with white or pale yellow or mauve, and I have tried to establish these combinations as much as possible once the meconopsis come out. Earlier, there are muscari and scillas and blue anemones, and also lungwort and forget-me-not, both marvellous ground covers; and later in August there are the agapanthus. These are a great standby, and I feel sorry for gardeners in the past who did not have the hardy strains we now enjoy. I have them planted by themselves along the top of a hundred-yard terrace wall, and they come all sorts of different blues and sizes. They demand full sun, and love the ash off bonfires, but otherwise are no trouble at all. In the wood they grow in a large patch in front of two tall *Eucryphia glutinosa*, and they are very beautiful together, with some plants of *Hydrangea* 'Blue Wave' as well.

One of the loveliest colour effects in the wood was unplanned. A few *Primula sikkimensis* crossed themselves with neighbouring *Primula ioessa* and the next three or four seasons there were hosts of seedlings of all colours from yellow and white to palest and deepest mauve. Sadly, I lost a great many of these during the hot dry summers of '75 and '76. One of the greatest virtues of *P. sikkimensis* is its heavenly scent. Indeed, all scented plants are welcome in my garden. We are lucky enough in our seaside warmth to be able to grow some of the tender sweet-smelling rhododendrons out of doors, and on a warm still day they can scent the whole wood. They are nearly all white, or palest flushed pink, and flower in June. Another delicious smell comes from the *auratum* lilies in August, which do very well in the wood as long as one can protect the bulbs from mice.

Then there are the magnolias. One of the sweetest is *M. wilsonii*. Wherever possible I have these planted close to a path, so that one may walk underneath the flowers which hang down from above. The king of magnolias is, I suppose, *M. campbellii*, its only disadvantage being that it is the opposite to *M. wilsonii* and turns its flowers up to the sky. The two trees here are both over forty foot tall, so one would really need to sit in a crow's nest to see the flowers properly. However, they are such a strong pink that they are very spectacular against the sky even from below. When their petals fall to the ground one can finger their toughness with a never failing sense of wonder and surprise. This year

92 and 93 Carpets of colchicums. From late August until October naturalized
C. speciosum album (left) *and* C. atrorubens (right) *give interest and colour*

94 and 95 *Part of the woodland garden. In 1930 three or four acres of acid soil were found. Lady Mary's father grew many rhododendrons, magnolias and acers, either from seed collected by the Asian expeditions of the '20s and '30s, or given from such famous gardens as Westonbirt and Wakehurst.* (Left) *An underplanting of Candelabra primulas among rhododendrons and azaleas.* (Right) Rhododendron barbatum

there are well over five hundred flower buds waiting to come out, and visitors stand gazing upwards, with cricks in their necks.

Yes, there are visitors – very much so. My father started opening the garden shortly after the last war, and it has been open to the public every day of the summer ever since, but only in the afternoons, so if one craves for solitude the morning is the time. It is in its way a real inspiration to know that so many people will see and appreciate it, and I find myself thinking a great deal about what they will like and expect. First of all, there must always be something to see. Secondly, a certain amount of tidiness is essential and I am extremely lucky to have two first-rate men and one woman to help to keep it up to standard. They do the mowing and the hedges and most of the pruning and weeding and all the heavy work (one is fully trained). I could not possibly keep the place going without them. The head man also does a lot of propagating in a mist unit, and we aim to keep ourselves going with cuttings as far as possible.

Almost all the visitors are perfectly delightful, enjoy it so much, and say such nice things. Among them are often a sprinkling of knowledgeable gardeners, and if I am lucky enough to be there when they come it is always interesting to talk, and to show them special plants, or ask advice. I have had many gifts sent to me afterwards from these experts. We do get the odd theft, but I believe this happens everywhere and I try not to plant things out until they have grown larger than pocket size.

The public start to come at Easter, when the place is covered with daffodils. There must be millions of them naturalized in the grass or under trees, all planted in drifts of single varieties. When I was a child this was our main autumn occupation. After the daffodils are over, one of the prettiest sights is nearly an acre of rough grass where every year mixed tulips come up, looking like the fields in a

75

96 and 97 *A corner of the wild garden in autumn and spring. A fine*
Cercidiphyllum japonicum *is underplanted with drifts of daffodils, narcissus*
and colchicums

Botticelli painting. Every autumn I put in one hundred new bulbs to keep them going, and they flower for three or four years before dying out. This piece of ground becomes a hayfield after that, with Ox-eye daisies, clover and poppies. I do not have it cut until July. Late in August a carpet of colchicums come up, both mauve and white, and these go on until the beginning of October. This piece of rough grass is one of my favourite bits of the garden, with a character all its own.

It is impossible to have a permanent favourite place, as the garden is always changing, and varies from season to season. Perhaps this is just as well, or the other parts might not get proper attention. I find I get ideas only when I am 'contemplating', and not actively working. This is very pleasant, as it gives one an excuse to wander through the various corners according to what is out, what the weather is like, or what the particular problem of the moment happens to be. Perhaps it is a gap to be filled, or a group to be re-arranged, or a new colour to be introduced. I have already said I love blue, but I also very much like pale pink or mauve, also yellow and white. But one cannot garden exclusively with pale colours, and even *Kniphofia* 'Lord Roberts' has its place of honour in September, magnificent spikes of fiery red planted in a mass all by themselves. Some of the brilliant red rhododendrons are splendid and spectacular, especially if they can be isolated in their own green setting. The public certainly loves a good splash of colour, so one cannot do without it.

When dealing with rhododendrons you must think well ahead, and I have been slow to learn this, but luckily they don't mind being moved. In fact, there is always a good deal of 'carriage exercise' going on in the autumn. Ten years after they have been planted, they have become quite a different shape, let alone size, and it is not always easy to foresee how they will fit into their surroundings. Some are worth growing for themselves, and I think this is true of most of the big-leaved varieties. They become points of architectural importance, and not only are their flowers magnificent, but their young foliage shoots are beautiful, pale green powdery rockets shooting straight up to the sky.

Shape is as important to a garden as colour, if not more so; different kinds of leaves play an enormous part. So do different kinds of greens, through all the shades from the blue-green of *Hosta* leaves and the gentle grey-green of *Pittosporum*, to the dark shiny richness of hollies and camellias. You can only achieve what you want through trial and error.

98 *In the woodland garden, vivid blue meconopsis grow through white and yellow flowered shrubs*

99 *Kniphofia 'Lord Roberts' has its place of honour in September*

Other people's gardens are to me the greatest possible help in trying to design my own, and I have shamelessly borrowed from many of them. Indeed, visiting other gardens is almost as delightful as being in one's own, and this goes for every type, large or small, from Cornwall to Inverewe. There is nothing more stimulating than other people's experiments and ideas, successes and failures. It is far the most satisfactory way of meeting new plants, much better than the shows, which are beautifully but artificially staged and give you quite the wrong impression of what something is going to look like once you have got it home.

Here at Howick there is always something to see, from the carpet of snowdrops in February right through to glorious autumn colour in October and November, all planted before my day. But perhaps the peak months are May and June. I am happy to say that a charitable trust has now taken over the ownership of the garden, so I hope it will survive in spite of the difficulties ahead. I am to continue looking after it as long as I am able to do so.

Mary Howick

St Nicholas
Richmond
Yorkshire

The Lady Serena James's Garden

ST NICHOLAS is an old garden made by Robert James, my late husband, at the beginning of the century. He was particularly interested in plants from the East and gradually a Nepalese jungle began to take over the rock garden. He subscribed to the expeditions to Western China and Nepal and got seeds of species rhododendrons. This meant cart-loads of leaf mould and peat as the soil is limestone rock. These rhododendrons were all numbered when they were first planted and are rather a unique collection of rare species now grown tall and intermingled, looking much as they would in their native land.

I came on to the scene in 1923, loving flowers, loving weeding, bored with long Latin names and with high-powered gardening friends, but with no say in the planting or layout. However, I did annex a small kitchen garden behind the privet hedge which was known as MY garden and still is.

With love and care we carry on and I find that I cannot bear to be away from what is a garden of

100 Moisture-loving plants on the slope near the house at St Nicholas. This was originally part of the rock garden

101 *Rose 'Bobbie James'. This famous climbing rose covers the whole of one side of the house*

102 *Part of the collection of species rhododendrons showing* Rh. *'Elizabeth'*, Rh. desquamatum *and* Rh. *'Humming Bird'*

great charm. It is open daily and I enjoy people coming round, they are appreciative as it is unique and has an atmosphere of great repose.

There have been only two head gardeners since St Nicholas was created and many gardens in England have been stocked by plants from here. My husband's advice was, 'give away a good plant, throw away a bad one', which I as caretaker of this wonderful garden continue to do when possible.

Serena James

103 *Part of a border. Here and in the main border some of the old shrub roses collected from cottage gardens, churchyards and elsewhere are still grown. When the garden was remade by Robert James some 80 years ago, it had a typical Victorian layout, with a conservatory attached to the house*

Coach House, Little Haseley, Oxfordshire

Mrs C. G. Lancaster's Garden

BEING BORN and bred a Virginian when Virginia was a poor state, I am partial to gardens of my childhood, which meant the survival of the fittest. Old Virginia gardens were never of the English landscape school, but based on seventeenth- and early eighteenth-century gardens, where boxwood was greatly valued, herbaceous borders unknown and flowers and vegetables intermingled. Light and shade and bone structure are the things I value most in a garden. I am not a horticulturist and delight in a hollyhock in the front and a violet at the back! I like common plants best. Abundance is all important as this hides mistakes. It is the ambience that I look for in a garden with a touch of sadness and nostalgia. I certainly have that now.

Nancy Lancaster

104 *A spectacular phalanx of roses at Coach House*
105 (Below) *The formal box garden has four weeping mulberries, and the beds are filled with Jackman's blue rue*

11 Cavendish Avenue
London
NW8

The Hon. Mrs Mark Lennox-Boyd's Garden

MY CHILDHOOD was spent in Italy and although I regarded my mother's stubborn pursuit to make a garden in the coldest, most wind-blown area I have ever known as rather useless, I did adore the wild flowers growing in abundance in the Sabine Hills north-east of Rome. I still delight in our fields there, carpeted with *Stachys lanata* and creeping thymes; verbascums are dotted around, dorycniums, helichrysums and genistas grow between the rocks. The oak woods are brilliant with cyclamen in September and primroses in the spring.

It was only when we came to live in England that I realized what fun gardening could be in a country where there are no extremes of temperature and where even the smallest cottage garden can display the most exquisite range of plants. With this growing fascination my eyes were opened to the countryside itself.

My practical experience in gardening started when I bought our present house in London about thirteen years ago. There was nothing particularly interesting about the layout of the garden, but it had immense possibilities. The big chestnut, the pear trees along the walls, and the sycamores and limes at the end of the garden, provided tremendous structure and a feeling of being in the country. In the spring I am often woken by the birds. One morning I even had the excitement of seeing an enormous mallard sitting on the lawn being stalked by our cat.

I started with no knowledge whatsoever of planting or designing. I read with enthusiasm all the books I could lay my hands on, became a member of the R.H.S. and went religiously to all their shows. I visited as many of the famous gardens as I could, took books of notes and kept my eyes and ears open for advice and new ideas.

106 Mrs Lennox-Boyd's London garden. Near the house are massed pots of foliage plants and a pergola planted with a Wisteria multijuga *'Alba'*

81

One of my girl friends who was a marvellous gardener, introduced me to all the old English favourites, such as old fashioned roses, lavenders and pinks. A more experienced lady gardener advised me what to do with a long bleak bed I had dug along the length of the south-east facing wall: she told me to plant evergreens for structure. I didn't understand what she meant, and of course did nothing about it. Another well-known gardener told me to imagine a garden in black and white, because if the structure and the planting are good in a black and white photograph then the design is good. That observation also went straight over my head. I now see exactly what these two friends meant. I always keep their advice in mind as both things are essential when making a garden.

I think you need a permanent structure, foliage or different shapes and colour, and you must always imagine the garden in three dimensions when designing it, and be aware of the seasonal changes. In a small London garden this is more difficult, so you must concentrate on a good foliage effect all the year round. I like to mix a great variety of grey plants in with other shrubs. Then, when August comes, and all the subtleties of the different greens disappear, they provide the contrast so badly needed in those depressing, heavy days. That is when I long to be in a cool, green, severe, Italian classical garden with no ornament other than statues and running water. That is the month when gardening in London has exhausted itself. No Clematis or Japanese anemones can relieve the feeling of depression brought about by the sight of overspent roses and faded euphorbias.

I have changed the garden three times and learnt a great deal through my countless mistakes. The first constructive step to success was the round hedge three-quarters of the way down the lawn. *Malus floribunda* and the white Judas tree grow on either side of the hedge, giving height and a feeling of seclusion to the lawn within. In the centre I planted a mass of Iceberg roses surrounded by lavender 'Hidcote', to create a focal point from the drawing room window. The white roses and the dark hedge form a view of simplicity and coolness, an inviting resting point when walking from the rambling, colourful area nearer the house towards the woodland garden. I constantly expanded the beds to take in new plants, much to the chagrin of my young daughter, who complained bitterly that she had nowhere left to play. My enthusiasm for gardening grew until it became my full-time commercial occupation, and I knew enough about plants and trees to design other people's gardens.

I cannot say precisely what has influenced me most. I think I have an eye for space and structure and this is certainly because of my Italian background. As for the general feeling and planting I think that Tyninghame has played a large part in moulding my ideas. Yet it was in a cottage garden in Berwickshire that I first began to understand the subtleties of planting.

After the initial planting, most of the shrubs were

107 The focal point seen from the drawing-room window. 'Iceberg' roses surrounded by Hidcote lavender lighten the scene

108 Looking back towards the house. A long stretch of lawn is bordered by shrub roses. The tall trees create a feeling of seclusion

either given to me or bought on the spur of the moment. Generally I don't grow plants from cuttings. London gardening is impatient. Cities have a different pace. It is such fun to buy an instant clump of hostas or a big *Cornus mas*. Raising plants from seed is a different matter, and I find it tremendously exciting to watch a seedling emerge and grow into a plant.

Our garden is not static. Plants get moved around. *Syringa velutina* with its delightful small mauve flowers grows prettily just between *Hebe subalpina*. This small Korean lilac is now three feet tall and the hebe has grown around it like a pale green frilly skirt. I also love purple leaved fennel growing next to pale, flesh-pink Canterbury rose 'Chaucer' and the double white Scots briars, in a grey border with *Hosta sieboldiana* 'Elegans'.

Last autumn I planted a *Wisteria multijuga* 'Alba' on a pergola. The flowers are white, tinted lilac, in long racemes. I adore wisterias, they bring back memories of childhood. In particular, I remember hiding in a wooden summer house covered in wisteria during one of the bomb attacks on Rome during the last war. I felt so safe and snug and the juice in the tips of the flowers was deliciously sweet.

Arabella Lennox-Boyd

83

Balbithan House
Kintore
Aberdeenshire

Mrs Mary McMurtrie's Garden

VISITORS TO Balbithan invariably remark on its tranquil atmosphere. It is a *green* garden, and green is restful to the eye. Of course there is colour but on the whole it is gentle and restrained while, enhanced by so much green, the occasional vivid patch of brilliant colour is unexpected and stimulating.

The main layout of the garden is still in the traditional Scots manner with straight paths dividing it and with a walk all round the sides. The restoration of an old ruinous wall which runs down its length has been an outstanding success, it has 'made' the garden. No longer is it flat and uninteresting, all visible at a glance, but now with the high wall, with yew and rose hedges and flowering trees, it is divided into a number of smaller gardens and pleasant vistas.

The planting is partly a compromise, because as well as many old garden plants that are now rare, I grow alpines, gentians, and have a peat bank with heaths. These are mostly grown for the nursery which helps to keep the garden going.

My aim has been to make the garden in keeping with the old turreted house; thereby giving the house a garden that belongs to it.

Mary McMurtrie.

109 At Balbithan House, raised beds filled with dianthus and auriculas edge a paved area. Behind is the original garden wall, rebuilt to incorporate the coping stones, and the square gateway with its heavy lintel

110 *An enclosed garden. Three Irish junipers,* Juniperus communis 'Hibernica', *make an effective focal point at the end of the path. On each side, the borders are filled with self-sown* Aquilegia 'Hensol Harebell', *carpeting phlox and campanulas*

111 *A stone wall surmounted by troughs where* Saxifraga lingulata 'Albida' *grow profusely between the crevices*

85

Westwick Cottage, Leverstock Green, Hertfordshire

Mrs Donald Macqueen's Garden

WE BOUGHT two four-hundred year old cottages just after the war. They were about to be condemned which will give you an idea of the state they were in. They stood almost in the centre of a two acre site, amidst a desolate mess of cans, bottles, old tyres and bits of farm machinery. We slowly cleared away the debris and worked on a three year plan which I may say I am still working on thirty years later!

Before we did any planting I stood in each room in the house and decided where to place the borders. Having cleared and turfed the front garden, we planned a border which we could look along from the house. I am a firm believer that borders look much better viewed from the end as they run into the distance, than if looked at head on, so to speak.

Naturally, we chose plants that were suitable for me to cut and use not only in the house, but for my many lectures on flower arranging. I have to admit that I started growing things to cut and having grown them became a gardener and now can hardly bear to cut anything!

Sheila Macqueen.

112 *A mixed border of perennials and annuals at Westwick Cottage, where Mrs Macqueen grows a great variety of plants especially chosen for her floral arrangements*

113 (Above) *A stone urn filled with nicotiana, pelargoniums and lobelia, as beautiful as any cut flower arrangement*

114 (Above, right) *A stone trough in front of the house*

115 (Right) *Staddle stones under a flowering cherry Prunus 'Kwanzan'*

The Old Rectory, Burghfield, Berkshire

Mrs Ralph Merton's Garden

FROM THE very beginning, I knew that I wanted to make an 'old' garden full of sweet-smelling cottage plants, aromatic herbs and shrubs, and voluptuous cabbage roses, dripping with enough scent to waft me nostalgically back to my childhood. This would create the proper setting for our eighteenth-century house, with its lovely old pink bricks and inviting feeling of warmth and welcome. It must have been the home of many happy old rectors and their contented calvesfoot-jelly-making lady wives.

When we bought the place in 1950 the garden was an almost blank canvas. Fortunately I found I could grow ericaceous plants even though the few flower beds consisted mostly of solid London clay which became rock-hard and full of cracks in summer and saturated in winter.

I soon fell under the spell of Sissinghurst and Vita Sackville-West, who fired me with enthusiasm and gave me wonderful ideas on plants and plant association. I discovered that not only do yews grow quickly if you give them a good start but that, to my amazement, I was married to the best yew-hedge trimmer in the business, whose sculpted masterpieces set off my herbaceous borders to perfection. These borders incidentally are never dug, as I read somewhere that the borders at the Botanical Gardens in Edinburgh have not seen a spade for nineteen years. Mine flower ceaselessly starting with daffodils, tulips, irises, paeonies, lupins, poppies and delphiniums. Phloxes, polygonums, Michaelmas daisies and Japanese anemones are interspersed with white daisies, erigerons, heleniums, crambes, rudbeckias, salvias, day lilies and kniphofias. You name them, they are all there in one glorious great jumble.

I then discovered those delightful books written by the late Margery Fish and began filling every square inch of the garden with hellebores and other spring plants and bulbs. From that time on I was lost and became a rapacious, insatiable plant collector, who, if she acquired *one* double primrose, had to have them all; *one* old garden pink, had to have at least twenty more; *one* lovely scented violet, would not rest until she had 'the Czar' tucked up in bed with 'the Princess of Wales' and all his other sweet-smelling lady friends. I never realized what potent, heady Barbara Cartland stuff plant association could be!

A helpful plumber who used to visit the garden regularly on open days asked me if I would like some old china sinks. I visualized a sink garden with a *few* tastefully tufa-covered troughs to protect a *few* rich and rare treasures that would otherwise certainly be lost in the hurly burly of the main garden . . . he brought me *thirty-one*! Now, besides my fifteen-sink sink garden, I am making a sink-surrounded

116 *The main pond in spring time in the garden at The Old Rectory. A beautiful Roman statue of Antinous dominates the scene. One hundred and thirty-five large elms have had to be felled recently and their place is now taken by new shrubberies and species rose gardens*

herb garden. The sinks are marvellous for restraining mints and other land-grabbers, and they grow Mediterranean plants that need very sharp drainage to perfection, or as near to perfection as you can get in our average summer.

The 'pleasure grounds' are giving me more and more pleasure as I add orchards, species rose gardens and shrubberies to replace the one hundred and thirty-five large, diseased elms that had to be felled, leaving us very exposed to the outside world. Luckily I still have another few acres up my sleeve, so in time we hope to be able to get back to our head-in-the-sand oasis life five miles from the centre of Reading.

I have one full-time gardener, another who comes ten hours a week to mow in the summer, and to hedge, ditch and saw up logs in the winter. Having about six of our twenty-six acres under some sort of cultivation, you can see that I have very little time for lolling about by our swimming pool, especially as I am now afflicted with 'propagation-itis' and have to take cuttings of everything. This entails endless frames and cutting beds, and eventually new places to house my surprisingly high proportion of successes! I cannot bear to throw any plant away, and must always find it another home either with me or with some kind, adoptive parent.

I am often asked to name my favourite flower but as every plant in its season is my 'heart's delight' from winter cyclamen, to the glorious rose explosion in June, from the intoxicating midsummer Regale lilies to the first hesitant stylosa iris at the end of the year, I find the choice impossible. Ferns are one of my passions and I tuck them in everywhere as they seem to put up with much more spartan fare than some of my more pampered beauties. They definitely have a quiet charm of their own and flower arrangers dote on them.

I am lucky enough to have three natural ponds. One is planted with gunneras, rheums, *Osmunda regalis* and other moisture loving ferns, and I have had to erect a barricade of tall bamboos to hide yet more ravages of the wretched Dutch Elm disease. The second pond is the main one with a lovely Roman statue of Antinous standing in the middle. Since the real Antinous committed suicide by drowning himself in the Nile, the statue is in the right place. The third pond where the geese and

117 A corner of the sink garden   *118 A curved bed full of quiet-toned herbaceous plants*

119 A view of the 18th-century house through the long double herbaceous borders

mallard frolic is in a different part of the garden altogether, beyond the kitchen garden and the new orchards, and here I am planting up a collection of willows, poplars and alders, purposely leaving it rather wild for the water fowl.

The garden is maturing and changing all the time and I love it to distraction! Roses are everywhere; the summer evenings are drenched in the scent of lilies, jasmines, tobacco plants, honeysuckles and other romantic spell-binders. I even have pots of ginger, heliotrope, verbena, and orange and lemon blossom to beguile me as I sit and sip my drink on the terrace.

My garden has to seduce me with heavenly smells, soothe me with cool, muted colours, fascinate me with the ever-changing parade of plants as season succeeds season. I forget about the visiting dogs who kill a choice treasure with one well aimed leg-lift; the squirrels who dig up my more expensive bulbs and munch them before my very eyes; the cows who occasionally gallop hock-deep over the lawns if the gate has been left open. I forget the seeds that decide not to germinate and the screaming red tulips that suddenly appear in a batch that was supposed to be pure white. I forget everything except the fact that I am a very lucky woman who lives for her garden, adores it, warts and all, and enjoys every moment of every hard-working day. What more can you ask of life?

Esther Newton

The Manor House, Bampton, Oxfordshire

Countess Münster's Garden

I SUPPOSE my interest in gardening began when I married and went to live in Austria at Schloss Wasserleonburg, Carinthia, a lovely place in marvellous surroundings close to the Italian frontier, with a wonderful climate. Then in 1936 we returned to live at Send Grove in Surrey. Although it had a good kitchen garden, with beautiful old red brick walls, the rest was very overgrown, and quite a challenge. The soil was acid, so we could grow plants and shrubs of all sorts. It had great charm.

In 1942 my husband and I moved to Shropshire, a beautiful part of England, where we had a farm. The children's nanny and I became the gardeners. This was a real apprenticeship and I learnt much about sowing and planting. The garden was mostly vegetables and fruit.

We came to Bampton in 1948, a lovely Oxfordshire village in the flat Thames valley, only a few miles from the beginning of the Cotswolds. Both house and garden were very attractive. I realized that the garden, because it was so flat, had to be broken up into rooms and vistas. I am sure I envisaged rooms similar to those at Sissinghurst and Hidcote, though on a smaller scale as my garden is only about five acres, two of which are kitchen garden, orchard and picking garden. In the kitchen garden are glasshouses and Dutch lights full of plants, for we sell both usual and unusual varieties.

The soil is limey and we have to feed our borders with compost and leaf mould in the autumn. In the spring we use general fertilizer. I am used to alkaline soil, as I was brought up in Gloucestershire and spent a good deal of my time weeding! My mother thought grass seed was too expensive and unnecessary, and a major task was to pull or dig up grass weeds from all over the garden and plant them close to each other. They grew and spread and eventually could be mown, and became a very good lawn. Quite inexpensive, providing your gardeners are your children!

120 A bold clump of Lysimachia punctata *growing by the pond of Countess Münster's garden. A weeping willow,* Buddleia alternifolia, *and plants with striking leaves are used effectively*

92

121 *A massed display of* Crocus tomasinianus. *The church tower dominates the garden from many points*

Underneath the many mature trees at Bampton are masses of snowdrops and aconites, carpets of *Crocus tomasinianus* and sheets of daffodils, *Narcissus* and *Tulipa multiflora*. A pleached lime avenue leads west to one of the kitchen garden gates, designed in Chinese Chippendale style. There is a break in the middle of this avenue: to the right you see the front door and attractive eighteenth-century 'Gothic' porch, to the left you look south down a wide grass path. On either side of this path are herbaceous borders, behind them another narrow grass path, then a yew hedge, about five feet high, with tall Irish yews coming up every six yards. How lucky that these yew hedges and the pleached lime avenue were planted a long time ago. These borders, which I keep full from spring to autumn, look good because of the background of the dark yew hedges, and my narrow grass path is invaluable when working at the back of them.

93

122 Spring colour: Prunus serrulata 'Amanogawa' *and daffodils flank the path to the loggia*

123 Colour in high summer: many gardeners consider that these borders are among the best in England

There is a lot of colour in my garden, but I think that evergreen and grey plants are important, because they remain the same throughout the year. I like to see euphorbias, hellebores, hypericums, rue, senecio and santolina.

Yew hedges also serve as the walls of two rooms that we made. Coming up from the front gate, one room on the left is round and everything in it is white and silver. In the middle a pleasure dome, made of treillage, has *Clematis* 'Marie Boisselot' and the white everlasting pea, *Lathyrus latifolius* climbing up over it, and *Epilobium glabellum*, a willow herb with creamy white flowers, at its feet. There are four silver weeping pears, *Pyrus salicifolia* 'Pendula', white roses and lilies.

The other side of the drive was originally a small paddock with a handsome sycamore tree and a pony. The paddock was full of weeds and nettles so we grew potatoes and vegetables until the weeds had gone, and then sowed grass seed. This was tidy but rather dull, so after a time my sister, a very good gardener and neighbour, helped me design two quite large beds, the one nearest the sycamore taking the shape of the tree's shadow. These beds are mostly full of shrubs and some roses, buff coloured, yellow and cream, and a lovely tall broom, *Genista cinerea*, which has such elegant and fragrant golden flowers. There are clumps of grasses as well: Bowles' golden grass, and a tall, striped one called *Miscanthus sinensis* 'Zebrinus', also *Festuca ovina glauca*. To keep it that lovely blue-green colour one should divide it at least twice a year and then replant the divided pieces close to the others, and they become good fat clumps.

A year or two later I thought a pond would look attractive. This was fairly easy, as our farm tractor dug out a very shallow bowl and tipped the soil onto an existing bank, only a few yards away. A local builder concreted the bottom and the sides. The trick is to fold back at least two feet of turf then, when the pond is finished, the turf gets pushed back over the sides and into the pond, hiding the concrete edges. The bottom is obscured by a collection of dead leaves, mud, weeds, water lilies and goldfish!

My husband was abroad when I created the pond. He was amazed when he returned and said, 'But Rothschilds gave up making lakes a long time ago!' It looks as if it has been there for ages, and a weeping willow almost weeps into the water.

Beside the house is another garden room bounded by a tall wall and yew hedges. I made four L-shaped beds inside with Hybrid Tea roses coming out of bare earth; they were horrible. These roses were transplanted to the picking garden and now there are three standard Ballerina roses in each. Under them are clumps of blue and pink lavender, rock hyssop, apple mint, green and silver thyme, golden origanum, paeonies, *Santolina*, *Salvia officinalis* 'Aurea', *Chrysanthemum densum*, and a few clumps of red-and-white striped tulips which burst through in the spring.

The border under the tall wall is filled with a mixture of shrubs and shrub roses and that lovely vine *Vitis coignetiae* climbs up and along the wall. Here I have a very large 'Roseraie de l'Hay', one of the best shrub roses, also 'Frau Dagmar Hastrup' and *gallica* 'Complicata', which has pink single flowers, simple, *not* complicated. In the middle of this garden is a sundial, surrounded by paving and silver and gold thyme: Time against thyme.

I put paving stones round the east and south sides of the house, leaving gaps for fuchsias, *Convolvulus cneorum* and *C. mauritanicus*, *Geranium sanguineum lancastriense*, *Ceratostigma plumbaginoides* and other treasures. Summer and winter jasmine and a great many roses grow up the sides of the house, and a prolific honeysuckle hides one of the drainpipes. On each side of the front door is a large bush of rosemary, and behind one is a *Ceanothus* 'Puget's Blue', this wonderful plant comes from America. Beside it is a yellow Banksia rose. On the left side of the door is a very old, very large wisteria, which is wonderful if one can prevent the birds taking the buds. The only way is to cover the branches, by the end of January, with Scaraweb. We always used the black, now we can only get white, so we have to dye it. The birds can obviously see white and are not scared, but the dark stuff frightens them.

124 The rose garden beside the house — standard 'Ballerina' roses and alternate bushes of blue and pink lavender. The surrounding beds contain hyssop, apple mint, and green and silver thyme

125 *The buttressed wall that separates the pleasure garden from the kitchen garden*

One imagines they do not see it, but they probably feel it on their feet, wings and beaks. A few yards further on at the entrance to a small, paved and cobbled patio are two cherry trees flanking the path. Here is a loggia, half covered with *Clematis armandii*. On the right, stone steps with iron bannisters lead up to a room in the house. In the summer, camellias and fuchsias in large pots stand at the foot of these steps. Opposite is an opening into the walled garden. Here a *pièce d'eau*, which does not look like a bathing pool, but is, has paving round it, and lead statues at the four corners.

Behind the pool, there is an orangery with gothic windows, which came from the park at Wilton. In summer the paving in front of the orangery has pots of daturas and agapanthus, and the vine *Vitis* 'Brandt' clambers upwards. On either side grow *Robinia* 'Frisia' trees, with rich golden-yellow leaves. There were two large walnut trees; both now dead and removed because of honey fungus. The south-facing wall is lower, and as it had shade from the walnut trees it had no plants in front or up it. I put a bed of Irish ivy, *Hedera* 'Hibernica', as ground cover in front of this wall, which is not allowed to grow higher than two feet.

One can leave this pool garden either the way one came in, or through another Chinese Chippendale style gate, facing west. This is not always easy to open because the beautiful *Clematis* 'Etoile Rose' spreads and hangs over the top, and as it is difficult to propagate, I try to avoid disturbing it too often. The other side of the gate has an unusual everlasting pea with apricot coloured flowers, called *Lathyrus rotundifolius*. Having successfully left the pool garden without spoiling 'Etoile Rose', go towards the spring garden, with bulbs and plants under beech, silver birch and a large *Cornus mas*.

Dominating the garden is Bampton church spire, beautiful and tall. I see it from my windows, from the walled garden, and best of all, just off centre as I look along my herbaceous borders. Some of the plants for these borders, as well as the ones that go on sale, are propagated and potted by our very splendid head gardener, Roy Holtom, who has been here twenty-seven years, and by Brian Loder who has been here twenty-one years. I am lucky they are so exceptional.

Peggy Munster

Rosemoor, Torrington, Devonshire

The Lady Anne Palmer's Garden

MY PARENTS bought Rosemoor as a fishing lodge in 1923 and much of my early childhood was spent here or at the family home in Norfolk. During the 1930s we were in New Zealand, so it was not until after the last war that my husband and I came to settle here more permanently.

Rosemoor garden covers an area of about seven acres, and is situated in the valley of the river Torridge on heavy clay in a frost pocket. What a place to start a garden although the setting is ideal with wooded hillsides to the north and east and some fine old hardwood trees to the south. These create a framework for newer plantings and afford some measure of protection from damaging winds, except those from the north-west which come blasting up the valley with little to stop them, searing any plants which happen to grow in their path.

In response to the tough weather conditions the garden is now mainly composed of hardy trees and shrubs. My very first planting was made as a result of an expedition with a trailer and Land Rover to my mentor's garden in Kent, to collect maple and cherry seedlings as well as 'layers' from his choice rhododendrons. I always remember that amongst the gifts was a piece of that very lovely *Paeonia mlokosewitschii* which was well chewed by our labrador puppy before it could be retrieved and planted. Remarkably it survived and has grown into a clump which flowers fleetingly each year, its pale yellow single blooms briefly surpassing anything else in the garden. This, the first of many gifts of plants, brought home to me the value of increasing suitable species, particularly rhododendrons and their relatives, by layering. Layering not only provides presents for other enthusiasts but also ensures the continuity of the plant on its own roots, thus ruling out the risk of suckers which are a major hazard with grafted plants for if the suckers are neglected they can take over the scion completely. Provided a fairly thin branch is growing near the base of the parent plant, it is the easiest thing in the world to put down a layer. The

126 Prunus sargentii *at Rosemoor. Lady Anne has planted bold groups of wild cherry species from the Far East*

97

127 The woodland garden in spring. Banks of wild primroses lighten the shadier areas

128 The original clump of Paeonia mlokosewitchii *growing under* Acer palmatum *'Senkaki'*

branch can be pinned down with the help of a forked stick, a little peat and sand heaped over the peg and a heavy stone placed on top of the peg. The same method can be employed with a branch higher up a stem, but this does entail fixing a box of soil in position where the branch can be set into it.

As my knowledge of plants increases, I realize more and more how little I really know, but one of the fascinations of a garden is that one continually learns and looks ahead, planning and planting new things. In my earlier days I made many visits to what could now be termed 'old-fashioned' nurseries where, at suitable seasons, a selection of the best forms for flower, autumn colour and so forth could be made by a label tied to the plant of one's choice, for delivery later. Now such nurseries seem hardly to exist and instead plants are selected from garden centres and taken away at will, as it is entirely uneconomical to allow employees in a nursery to spend long hours with a customer. It used to be such fun though, to discuss one's projects with an enthusiastic nurseryman. When I was planning Rosemoor another ploy of mine was to visit good gardens to glean ideas for plant associations, and eventual sizes and design; this is to be highly recommended to anyone starting a garden of their own. Shows can also be helpful, but they have an artificial aura and personally I prefer to see plants growing in gardens or better still, in their natural surroundings in the wild. In no way do I intend to denigrate the value of horticultural shows and in particular those arranged by the Royal Horticultural Society, culminating in their great display at Chelsea.

I have been fortunate in being able to travel to several parts of the world with the express purpose of seeing indigenous flora in forests and parks, and I find this the most exciting aspect of horticulture. After such trips one can attempt to place plants in similar conditions to those in which they grow naturally. Wild-collected seedlings or seeds germinated and subsequently planted out, can be a constant and living reminder of a particular trip. By the same token, a plant which has been grown from a cutting from a friend's garden is a permanent reminder of that friend.

My propagating is a bit haphazard, especially as I have never acquired a greenhouse worthy of the name. Through the years I have made do with a leaking Victorian conservatory attached to the house, supplemented by some rather inadequate cold frames covered with polythene which blows off in the wind. Despite the failures, I have managed to propagate many plants and I still maintain that one of

129 A trough with Shortia soldanelloides *'Magna' is framed by* Hedera helix *'Buttercup'*

130 Evergreen azaleas overhung by Halesia monticola *beside a woodland path*

the greatest thrills of my life was to find roots on a hydrangea cutting at my first attempt.

It is difficult to name any family of plants growing at Rosemoor as my favourite for my interest ranges far and wide. Certainly woody plants predominate here and perhaps I should mention a few, such as my groups of a dozen each of the wild cherries from the Far East, *Prunus spontanea, P. sargentii* and *P. pubescens*, planted on one of the hillsides where their flowers look gay and joyous in the spring and their leaves colour vividly in the autumn. Growing amongst them are many exotic trees and, as my experience increases, I lean more and more towards planting rare species which may sooner or later be threatened with extinction in their natural habitats. There are far too many eucalyptus around – were I starting again I would not plant a single one. They look alien in our damp northern climate and need the hot arid conditions of their native country. Having said that, I must add that they are really very decorative, particularly in winter when the leaves have come off the hardwoods and a little weak sun lightens up their blue-grey foliage.

Rhododendrons with their immense range of form, flower and foliage are a continual fascination, and I do not believe this great genus is really appreciated by the public at large. There is a rhododendron for every garden, great and small, especially if the soil is acid and there is reasonable protection from chilling winds. The young growth alone of many varieties is outstanding and the range of colour and form in the flowers must surely be exceptional in the world of plants. They are easy plants to move, even in flower, so one can cart them around the garden until the right site is found for their individual shape and colour.

Visitors come throughout the spring, summer and autumn as the garden is open daily. Although unforeseen interruptions can be annoying when one is gardening, I am only too glad to take people round if their visit has been planned beforehand. This is not only interesting, but can also be very useful as I often observe jobs such as ties which need letting out or plants which need staking that I normally pass by a dozen times without noticing. I always feel very ashamed when I see a tie practically cutting a stem in half which must have needed attention for months if not years.

A garden can be compared to the rooms of a house. Some people like to constantly shift the furniture around, others more conservative, like to leave it where it has always been. In a garden

99

132 (Above) Prunus sargentii in autumn

131 (Left) Prunus serrula. Its polished bark is a feature near the scree bed

changes can well be made and innovations are exciting, but require a great deal of forethought. For instance, as one's garden gets more crowded, it pays to become ruthless in discarding plants unworthy of their position. Although this entails difficult decisions I find that once the plants are actually on the bonfire, remorse is precluded by the anticipation of things to come. Sometimes I spend months thinking about a new area and sifting through advice from gardeners whose skill I respect, eventually reaching a decision. Alternatively it is flattering to be asked to give one's opinion on a design for another garden, but I always prefer to ponder over my reply and dislike giving instant advice. Except when our old kitchen garden was brought into the ornamental area no professional advice has been sought here. Probably those who know the garden will murmur 'better if there had', but it has grown like Topsy over the years as more plants were acquired.

Rosemoor is cared for by a full-time gardener, a student who more often than not comes from Holland to spend the summer months gaining practical gardening experience, and myself when other duties permit. I have many faults, but laziness is not one of them and when possible work from dawn to dusk – I am never happier than when working out of doors. I must confess, though, to many hours of despair and disappointment when things fail to progress as I had hoped. More and more I realize the importance of mulching with peat, leaf-mould or even sawdust, although with the latter nitrogen must be added and there is always the risk of encouraging honey fungus.

With ever-increasing labour costs and the owners' advancing years it is a matter for speculation how much longer gardens such as this can continue. Rosemoor is now a charitable trust but the income obtained from garden entrances, plant sales and the small endowment we were able to make when first forming the trust does not cover the running costs. It would be heatbreaking if the garden were to fail after all the time and labour expended on its development.

Anne Palmer

100

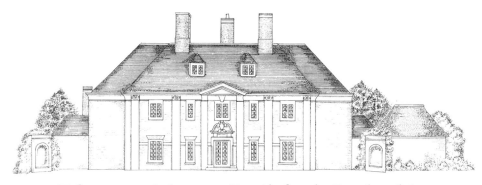

Ednaston Manor, Brailsford, Derbyshire

Mrs Stephen Player's Garden

EDNASTON MANOR was designed and built by Sir Edwin Lutyens for my father-in-law, W. G. Player. It was completed by 1920, having been started in 1912, with very little work being done during the war years. It never became the family home, but was visited frequently by them.

When we came to live here in 1948 there was this beautiful Lutyens house and the foundations of a promising garden. The chestnut and plane tree avenues and the yew and holly hedges were all thirty years old. Besides these there were four *Cedrus atlantica glauca* and two large beds of *Acer palmatum* and *Azalea* spp as well as various other shrubs. A bank of grafted hybrid rhododendrons sheltered the garden from the west. Unfortunately, the *Rhododendron ponticum* has taken over in a big way.

It was wonderfully exciting to come to a garden with light, well-drained, loamy, acid soil, ideal for all the lime-hating shrubs and ericaceous plants. Lilies too grow well. In fact, if you are lucky enough to have this type of soil, there is little you cannot grow. I find this a great joy as one has such freedom of choice. So here to me was a gardening paradise, apart perhaps from the climate, which is harsh.

The house and garden stand at about five hundred feet above sea level and the house faces south. You approach the house on arrival from the west side which is protected by semi-circular walls with three openings for the carriage drive. These walls form a forecourt.

Protection and shelter for a garden are the most important things. Wind destroys more trees and shrubs than any healthy frost. Unfortunately, having always loved gardening but never taken it seriously, I did not study the wind in this garden before I started planting, so it was ten years before I realized shelter belts must be planted on the north-west, north and north-east sides. A certain amount of shelter did exist, but wind does funny things and it was undoubtedly due to wind that some of our

133 The sheltered south-facing terrace. Brick paths edged with Derbyshire Hopton stone separate several small beds

*134 The approach to Ednaston Manor. Sir Edwin Lutyens designed a
semi-circular courtyard. The red brick walls are now completely rose-clad*

earliest plantings succumbed. It was not until 1960 that I became really enthusiastic and decided what I
wanted to create here. For the next few years I read every book, gardening article and catalogue I could
lay my hands on. I wanted to make my garden more beautiful, and to grow trees and shrubs that were
different. I think I am a collector rather than a garden designer. I had all the space and scope I needed.

I suppose however far sighted a gardener is, one cannot visualize quite what twenty years or so will
do to a garden. Without the help, support and advice of my husband, and of my gardener who came
here in 1951, and a great many arguments, I undoubtedly would have made many more mistakes. My
enthusiasm ran away with me. More and more trees, shrubs and plants kept arriving by every means
of transport. Finally, after several years of this 'planting bonanza' a halt was called or rather a 'cut
down', and a suggestion made that it might be a good idea to do some propagating ourselves and
perhaps a little selling in order to help pay for some of my enthusiastic buying. Of course this wasn't
easy, but once again, owing to our head gardener's help, the project was launched. New greenhouses
were erected and from a very slow and humble beginning a business has been built up and the garden
is now on its way to being self-supporting.

In the early days the garden was only open to the public once a year, but gradually it became
difficult to choose the best date so we opened more and more and now we are open virtually all the
year round. Sharing the garden with other people is very important to us. Having built up this
collection, a great deal of which is now mature, there would be little point if no one saw it. In this part
of England we are very isolated from the famous gardens, so I wanted people to be able to come here
and see what could be grown and what the shrubs and trees I had collected looked like when mature.

My garden is, I hope, of interest to everyone because there are so many different corners which can

135 The woodland garden in spring, filled with a fine collection of acid-loving plants

be related to almost any garden you can imagine, large or small, town or country. In many cases one can go into the selling area and buy in containers what you have seen, or order what you want for later delivery. The container grown plant has revolutionized gardening. It has created a form of 'instant gardening' which to my mind takes a great deal of the excitement away. To grow anything from seed is a huge thrill. To watch it germinate, potting it on until it is sufficiently mature to plant out, then the excitement of the first flower on your own seedling, is very rewarding. The same excitement exists when specimen trees mature, as we found with our *Davidia involucrata*, the 'Pocket Handkerchief Tree' which produced its white bracts for the first time fifteen years after planting. All this to me is 'gardening'. It requires patience, but the reward is enormous.

Here at Ednaston in the shrub and woodland parts, only hand weeding is done in order that as much regeneration as possible can survive. The excitement is tremendous when a special seedling is found, be it rose, shrub or tree. It is then carefully marked and when large enough moved either to a more suitable position or to the nursery to flower there to see if it has merit or is of no interest. Most, but not all thank goodness, are generally of the former variety!

The area we opened up which we now call the 'woodland garden' consisted of Scots pine trees which we thinned out as much as we dared as they had been planted to protect the house from the north wind. There was also a great deal of undergrowth in the form of brambles and elder. Regretfully, we made this garden in three stages, which has led to many planting mistakes, but we did it this way because we were waiting for the shelter-belts to grow up. This woodland area consists of grass paths leading round beds of shrubs under-planted with ground cover. Many of the trees have roses or *Clematis montana* growing up and through them. There are one or two rather poor specimens of grey cedars which look marvellous in the spring when the clematis are in flower. It is hard to describe, but very effective. In this area too, we have a collection of camellias which have done remarkably well, and I have now planted many more elsewhere in the wood. Amongst my collection of shrubs are a great number of viburnums which are marvellous both in flower and for autumn colour. The same goes for varieties of cornus.

In 1952 I was given a cutting of a fantastic rambling rose. It has grown to a prodigious height over the top of a large holly tree and down the other side. This is a marvellous sight in early July. Several more of them in other parts of the garden carry out various functions such as disguising a telegraph pole. I think it is very important to make use of some shrubs and trees as hosts for other climbers.

We longed for water in the garden, but where to make a pond that did not look totally out of place on top of our hill? A very successful solution was to make a 'dew pond' such as you see in many places in our local countryside. Now water drips from a large stone trough into the pool which we placed at the end of a stone path in a corner of the wood. The result seems very natural and has given us the pond we so much wanted. The overflow is used to make a boggy bed where primulas flourish.

The terrace on the south side of the house is my favourite part of the garden. You enter through doors from the east and west side. It is prettily designed with brick paths edged with Derbyshire Hopton stone flags and enclosed by walls with a summer house at each end. There are a dozen small beds of various shapes and sizes. Originally these were bedded out twice a year, but long ago I decided that this was very dull. So I planted a mixture of roses and shrubs with a few wallflowers, tobacco plants and geraniums according to the season.

This terrace is the most important part of the garden both in summer and winter as it is seen from so many windows of the house. I felt I must have a mixture that gave me both colour and interest during the greater part of the year. I have used China roses and a few of the dwarf Floribundas underplanted with hardy pinks, violas and many other plants. As this is naturally sheltered, and combined with the help of the recent mild winters, I have experimented with border-line 'hardy' shrubs which I have tucked in. It seems that if they survive their first Derbyshire winter, they become acclimatized and then enjoy life here. Close up to the house two *Carpenteria californica* are getting far too big, but they flower profusely and are evergreen so never look naked or ugly. I find the potentilla family useful, both the shrubs and plants, but the shrubs have either to be pruned or replanted fairly frequently to keep them a reasonable size. Another useful family for the late summer is *Caryopteris*. They must not be pruned until April, but in winter their stick-like branches look pretty covered in frost. Growing up this south side of the house I have roses with *Clematis* and various other climbers. They all seem to grow happily together in a fearful tangle, but it does help to have continuous flower and colour. The one thing I have had total failure with in this part of the garden is bulbs. They always seem to get eaten by somebody (I suspect mice), so I have ceased to struggle. In theory I try not to have anything over three feet on this terrace because of spoiling the view from the

house. The soil is good and strong and everything flourishes, so I have to be very ruthless and continually prune or move things to keep the balance right, which is fun because there is always the excuse to try something new.

On the east side of the house the design of the garden is architectural which includes terraces on different levels with steps leading from one to the other, formal yew hedges and lawns.

136 The chestnut avenue was planted in 1920. In spring it is carpeted with daffodils

137 The dewpond. A recent feature

138 The climbing rose 'Bantry Bay'

All this is entirely symmetrical. I find it difficult and rather forbidding instead of being warm and friendly. Therefore I have tried, with I hope some success, to alleviate this formality by planting a profusion of climbing roses together with various varieties of clematis and honeysuckle. Against the house I have *Rosa primula* entirely for the scent of the fern-like leaves. The flowers are single yellow and bloom early and only once. I have placed several stone troughs along the terrace walls containing alpine plants, for which I have a great deal of enthusiasm and do not find demanding.

I have also replaced some old beds of Hybrid Tea roses with various shrubs, plants and lilies. I am trying to have each bed a different colour, but I am not finding this quite as easy as I originally thought. Leading off the main lawn in this area is the lower garden where the main feature is a grass walk flanked by old-fashioned and shrub roses, with climbers, ramblers and various clematis trained to form a pergola, leading to a small pond and seat which in turn is flanked by a newly planted semi-circular tapestry hedge. The remainder of the lower garden is now used as a nursery and in a limited way for vegetables.

Luckily, adjoining this formality is the old orchard enclosed on two sides by a magnificent beech hedge. We have been able over the years to replace the fruit trees with many specimen trees and shrubs including a variety of magnolias. I have also made a rock garden here where I can grow my alpines.

My greenhouses, which are not extensive, are full of many varieties of 'house plants'. I have a large collection of the *Begonia* family, also many varieties of pelargoniums and geraniums which do so well indoors. I dislike picking and arranging flowers for the house, partly because I am lazy but mostly because I think they look so much better growing naturally.

The endless delight of a garden, no matter what size, is that you can always be altering and hopefully improving it. Over the years as I have learnt more about plants, I have become increasingly selective, but one thing is certain: I shall never be satisfied, so I shall never have finished my garden.

Jean Player

105

Ling Beeches, Scarcroft, West Yorkshire

Mrs Arnold Rakusen's Garden

MY EVOLUTION as a gardener began when I was four, and I still recall my delight in picking strawberry flowers in 'nanny's daddy's' garden! Later came school, where compulsory botany and Latin taught me enough to understand botanical Latin terms. The library provided for my interest in eighteenth-century art and politics, and further reading about men influential in the great landscape movement helped when I came to plan my own garden.

I had followed Theo Stephens, Vita Sackville-West and Clarence Elliott in the Sunday newspapers, then I began to read their books, also those of Gertrude Jekyll, A. T. Johnson, Michael Haworth-Booth, G. S. Thomas and others, all of whom made me realize my site was God's gift to a gardener. Margery Fish's *We made a Garden* ensured my determination to have a garden that would be interesting on every day of the year.

We are fortunate to have owned the same house and garden for thirty-four years, and I must now describe the place as it was when we came here after our marriage. The house had been built in 1938 in old plantations of beech, larch, Scots pine, rowan, birch and oak, once part of the Bramham Park estate. Large beech formed an avenue down the lane with undergrowth of bilberry, bracken and male fern. The soil was acid, as one would expect. The house stood in a small clearing on the two acre site with a rickety, stone path leading to the front door and the small 'lawn'. It was indeed romantic with its white-washed walls of old brick, and roof of old pantiles arched over by beech trees. But to things more practical!

The site is nearly five hundred feet above sea-level, the rainfall an average twenty-seven inches and prevailing winds south-westerlies. The thin soil is well drained, but leached by the trees. Worms were conspicuous by their absence and even leaf-mould pockets were few. The house had been well-placed on a slight elevation to the north-east of the site, the land gently sloping southwards, allowing frost drainage where no plants obstruct. On this charming spot I had been trying to grow a border of herbaceous plants and had built up a mound I called a 'rockery'. We soon found that the sun only shone on the garden when it was directly overhead.

In 1945 I engaged Fred as a gardener-handyman for two days a week. He and I spent hours digging out tree roots and rolling them to the bonfire. The trunks and branches were logged by my husband. As we began to enlarge the tiny garden I realized the need for topsoil which was then fifteen shillings per ton, delivered; peat bales were sixteen shillings. But I must hurry over the wasted years of growing the wrong plants to the exciting stage heralded by giving away my Hybrid Tea roses. I decided to follow Repton, to make the house sit on a platform, a terrace, and to take Haworth-Booth's advice to 'anchor the house to the site' by planting. Shirley Hibberd considers a terrace should be as wide as half the height of the house; mine nearly conforms, but appears less as plants have encroached. Terrace and lawn meet at a low dry-stone wall.

I had become a plantsman and working in the right direction at last, I found planning convenient from bedroom windows. Fred would move canes and ropes about, representing plants and paths, while I shouted 'towards Leeds', or 'towards Wetherby'. Thus we gradually extended westwards, planning the longest vista, east to west, to be seen when reaching the terrace from the drive. Here we built a brick wall, with canted sides, giving privacy from the drive and shelter for a seat; the rays of the setting sun in summer fall straight down the terrace, making this a favourite spot for pre-dinner drinks.

South-west of the extended, irregularly-shaped lawn we reluctantly felled a large beech and utilized the vast hole to make a pool, lined first with small stones – I became expert with a lump-hammer – and

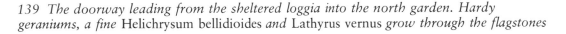

139 The doorway leading from the sheltered loggia into the north garden. Hardy geraniums, a fine Helichrysum bellidioides *and* Lathyrus vernus *grow through the flagstones*

140 Humulus lupulus '*Aureus*' growing up a Scots pine, one of the trees on the drive

141 *Silver foliage and yellow flowers surround a staddle stone near the house*

142 Clematis montana *festoons a pine, with Canadian hybrid lilac 'Bellicent' in the foreground*

then with waterproof cement, laid by professionals. As the pool lies south of my old 'rockery' (since replanted and re-christened 'the mound') it appears to be natural, as planting masks the southerly sloping ground. Despite the trees, it affords much pleasure, particularly to birds and mammals, having clear water and well-balanced life. *Orchis maculata* threads around the lawn margin, *Osmonda regalis* and its crested form flourish, as do other ferns, primulas and moisture-loving plants. Frogs and toads demolish my vast slug population, and we enjoy the birds attracted to drink and to bathe. Westwards a path widens into a stone circle on which is another seat – a pleasant spot on hot days, especially when *Rubus tridel* 'Benenden' flowers nearby.

Scents are important to me and I always give preference to scented forms of plants. I enjoy *Rhododendron luteum* for this; its autumn colour, too, is better than showier hybrids. I grow many herbs as part of the general scheme, and enjoy walking round the garden to collect marjoram, chives, fennel and thyme for cooking. Rosemary is within reach of the sitting-room window and I have several pots of mints near the kitchen door. Their aromatic oils help to keep away flies. I grow *Ptelea trifoliata* mainly for its scented flowers, like orange blossom, though now I wish I had chosen the golden form. However, my plant colours to butter-yellow in autumn, though never setting the beautiful seedpods seen further south. *Choisya ternata* is planted in woodland shelter. My old shrub roses and species are mostly scented, *R. filipes* 'Kiftsgate' now tops a forty foot Scots pine, making a dreamy sight and scent in August. *Philadelphus* 'Belle Etoile' grows near that delicious modern hybrid-musk rose 'Magenta'. Their combined scents are heady and the purple blotches on the former perfectly complement the dusky, mauvy-pink of the latter.

The south-facing house-wall shelters *Cytisus battandieri*; how I wish for more such walls. *Trachelospermum asiaticum* is another 'smellie' needing protection here. My many ivies which I grow on walls, dead trees and as ground cover, produce scented flowers and form an important part of the winter scene. There are tiny ones in the terrace troughs. One of my regrets is that I was unable to afford hollies years ago; by now they would have been mature and would help cut westerly ground-draughts.

This is still a shady garden, the trees filtering the winter sunshine, so I value pale foliage such as *Ligustrum ovalifolium* 'Argenteum', *Iris foetidissima* 'Variegata', *Pachysandra terminalis* 'Variegata' and *Lamium maculatum* 'Variegatum'. I learnt the hard way which of the golden-foliaged plants

108

retain their colour in shade. When choosing plants I put foliage first, enjoying the year-round bounty of broad-leafed evergreens.

Conifers are not very successful here, although a central focal point is *Chamaecyparis lawsoniana* which came as a babe from my husband's old home. *Pinus aristata*, *Abies koreana*, *Taxodium distichum* and *Metasequoia glyptostroboides* are among my treasures. Others started life in the troughs, and were moved as they outgrew their homes and sometimes moved yet again.

I regard flowers as a bonus to be kept within my rather strict colour scheme. Jarring colours spoil the harmony I have aimed for and enjoy, based upon the garden in June at foxglove time. Their pink and white spires in the woodland are the essence of this part. Those in unsuitable places are consigned to compost. Pale colours appeal, especially sulphur-yellow; I allow some red, but not modern orange-red. Strangely enough *Geum* × *borisii* looks superb with *Cotinus coggygria* 'Foliis Purpureis' and *Erysimum* 'Bowles' Mauve'. In autumn *Geranium collinum* rambles through low shrubs, picking up the colours of *Aster* × *frikartii*, hardy fuchsias and *Erica* 'H. E. Beale', 'Peter Sparkes' and *Cinerea* 'Lilacina'. Honesty continues the scheme in spring, adding its ethereal, silvery tones in winter.

I fell out of love with heathers and species rhododendrons years ago. Old 'iron-clads' shelter us on the boundaries. I cannot grow plants as collections, even ferns and grasses must fit into the general scheme. I sometimes think of the garden as a layer-cake – each part providing interest at several times of the year.

Ensuring this interest and supporting this heavy planting is the compost heap. I believe in feeding my plants, using bone-meal, sewage sludge, hop manure and farm-yard manure, but varying the fertilizer on each part. Leaf and bracken mould was used before neighbouring woodland was felled and sharp sand and grit help soil texture, but the main food is compost. We tried several methods for producing it, all of which resulted in putrefaction, rather than the desired decomposition by fermentation. However, Alwyn Seifert's book *Compost* ensured success; no activator is used, but plenty of woody material maintains an open texture, and the worms do the rest. Much peat goes into planting and mulching, paying a good dividend in times of drought. I never use inorganic fertilizers, as I believe soil structure to be of prime importance.

I confess that I enjoy giving pleasure to others and am delighted when people find the garden restful, especially those not aesthetically minded. I recall a man saying in wonderment, 'so many different greens'. Like Gertrude Jekyll I believe that green is a colour. Sometimes visitors say, 'you must be proud of your garden'; with humility, I must agree, but with reservations, being conscious of mistakes, such as our too-narrow stone paths. I would have liked a wider terrace too and a larger paved area by the

143 In the wood in early spring. Here Rhododendron praecox, Rh. *'Bo-Peep' are effectively associated with* Narcissus *'February Gold' and* Pachyphragma macrophyllum

144 *The sundial. Stone paths lead through luxuriant beds filled for year-long effect. There are foxgloves, verbascums,* Lonicera nitida *'Baggessen's Gold', the shrub rose Ferdinand Pichard, Rose 'Tom's pink' and evergreens for effect in winter*

loggia, even a larger loggia. In fact there are many things now too late to remedy. However, I am proud of having made the soil, the hard work involved has been rewarded. I have done, or helped with, every job except mowing (that great bore!) and I'm not interested in perfect lawns either.

Fred retired in 1972; Mr Gibson now comes five hours each week. Edinburgh trained, second of thirty at Mount Stewart, then head gardener at Dawyck, I knew him before illness forced him to retire from his nursery. To him I owe my ability to remove plants that have served their time. Also thanks to him I have learnt to wield the pruners, having previously been oblivious to plants past their prime. We spend happy hours arguing, yet finally agreeing; happy times, for me, listening to tales of gardening on the grand scale. Now a young contractor does occasional heavy work, but the garden ticks over while Mr Gibson and I plod on.

I have never exhibited plants and infrequently visit shows. Flowers are only a part of plants, plants part of gardens. It is the totality I enjoy, therefore I indulge in much garden visiting. I aimed to 'marry' house to garden, and some people are kind enough to say I have been successful; but how can eucryphias and embothriums from Chile, hebes from Australasia, rhododendrons from the Himalayas look natural in Yorkshire? To say nothing of hellebores from eastern Europe, and hostas and paeonies from China and Japan. I believe the word should be harmonious. I wanted to create a complete picture, with scenes from the windows forming parts of the whole at all seasons.

My appreciation is extended to all to whom I am indebted. My husband and children for their forbearance; my school, Malvern Girls' College; contributors and staff of *Country Life*, and the Northern Horticultural Society that I joined in 1953 and where I have worked for nearly twenty years. I am also indebted to the specialist nurserymen and women who keep rare plants going, in spite of economic difficulties, and to the Garden History Society through which I meet kindred spirits. Last, and most important, my grateful thanks go to all who open their gardens thus sharing enthusiasm, knowledge and pleasure in plants and planning with their fellow-gardeners and visitors.

Philippa Rakusen

Moyclare
Liskeard
Cornwall

Mrs Louis Reid's Garden

EVERY PLANT in such a small garden must have a very long period of beauty, of foliage as well as flower. I try not to have any bare earth at all and grow things in layers. A pendulous *Embothrium*, with a *Sophora*, create a shower of red and gold in June, while at the base I have a *Euphorbia wulfenii*, a variegated privet and a *Hebe*, which give colour and interest all the year. Climbing into the *Embothrium* is the violet rose Veilchenblau, which flowers in July, followed by the white *Clematis recta*. Camellias and rhododendrons with conifers give a tapestry effect and all have climbing roses and clematis growing up in them. This is the way things grow in nature and they flourish together.

I grow a great many tender plants, as I am always ready to try them, and they add interest to the garden. I am now experimenting with a 'spiky' bed where an unusual and colourful collection of variegated yuccas, phormiums, grasses, pampas and palms, tower over bulbs and spiky herbaceous

145 (Left) *Cordylines, phormiums and variegated yuccas are mixed with spiky herbaceous plants*

146 (Below) *Shrubs closely planted for wind protection. Greens, gold, grey and red give a lively tapestry effect*

plants. There are ferns under shrubs, double primroses, a collection of violets, and masses of plants of interest to flower arrangers, whose needs I am keenly aware of as I was a demonstrator for about twenty years.

I have been involved in the Horticultual Show world of the county ever since the war. From tiny village shows, to the big three day Cornwall Garden Society Show. I had a most interesting job after the war. The W.I. County Federation sent me to Denman College which was running a course on Village Shows and Flower Arrangement. When I got back I was on call for any village that wanted to start, or more often re-start a show that had died during the war. It was tremendous fun, and once they could stand on their own feet I was brought in as a judge.

I never had any children, the garden is my creation, and has all the love and attention a family would have had. An article I wrote for the R.H.S. Journal, or *The Garden* as it is now called, was entitled 'Cramming them in', and it is a fair comment, because that is just what I do, and what nature does as well.

Moira R. Reid.

148 *Not an inch of space is wasted.* Lapageria rosea *'Nash Court' with rose-crimson flowers envelops a golden berried* Pyracantha rogersiana *'Flava'*

147 (Left) *The north-facing border seen from the house is planted for spring with camellias, rhododendrons, azaleas and pieris, and enlivened in summer with clematis,* Tropaeolum speciosum *and herbaceous plants*

Chequers
Boxford
Suffolk

Miss Jenny Robinson's Garden

M Y RETURN home at the end of the war coincided with the departure of the last visible means of support in the garden. Innocently I volunteered to try to look after the flowery part. During the next tumultuous months I learnt two things. The first was that motor mowers are the spawn of the devil, and to be eschewed at all costs. The second was never to try to wield man-sized barrows of manure. I overturned one all over myself.

When I was house-hunting in 1958, a kind fate dropped particulars of Chequers through my letterbox and I felt at once that it was the house for me. What gardener would turn down two acres or so if they contained a suitable house, a walled garden and a stream?

In August, emerging from the titanic struggle of the move, I invested in a ruler and some squared paper and, armed with this equipment, I was to be found staring hopelessly at my broad and empty acres. (For the record, I discovered after only three years I had planted over two thousand different kinds of plants. It takes a lot to fill a garden.) There was hardly a tree worth having and my predecessors had a genius for putting things in the wrong place. The soil was thin and stony; ideal for a woman gardener. One can enrich it as one goes along and the all-important drainage is done for one. Soil samples sent to the R.H.S. brought the answer: 'Totally devoid of humus and a pH of 7–8.' The whole garden is on a barely perceptible slope to the stream, where of course the soil is alluvial.

The first stages began. Two brick paths were laid, one leading to the all-important cold frames where I do all my seed raising and rather primitive methods of propagation, and nearby I built some raised beds. I was given three months in which to remove plants from my old home.

149 (Left) The walled garden at The Chequers with its central lawn and well-filled borders. This west-facing bed has iris, hostas, Rosa chinensis 'Mutabilis' and Rosa rubrifolia

150 (Right) The climbing rose 'Paul's Himalayan Musk' envelops a Populus × regenerata with Genista aetnensis growing nearby

151 *Miss Robinson's garden is noted for fritillaries, a few of which are shown here.* (Top, left to right) *(a)* Fritillaria graeca thesallika, *(b)* Fritillaria tuntasia, *(c)* Fritillaria conica, *(d)* Fritillaria pyrenaica, giant form. (Bottom) *(e)* Fritillaria pontica, *(f)* Fritillaria pallidiflora, *(g)* Fritillaria verticillata, *(h)* Fritillaria acmopetala

For help I had a pensioner who came every morning. What luxury! Nowadays all the help I have is a fifteen-year old who mows the grass when the spirit moves him, and the good Mack who comes one afternoon a week. It is not enough.

To go back to that first autumn. I concentrated initially on the garden near the house, removing beds of Hybrid Tea roses in front of the windows and filling the space with a mosaic of low growing plants and shrubby thymes, acaenas, ballota and daphnes, with all sorts of dwarf bulbs spearing up between. In this patch I think I have succeeded in having something to look at every week of the year.

Up three steps which are adorned by pots of trailing geraniums and into the walled garden. Here I made the width of the beds equal to the eight-foot height of the walls, which seems the right proportion. The beds face north, south, east and west, and are over-flowing with a mixture of everything conceivable which will grow in my conditions. It is an ideal soil for bulbs. Sir Cedric Morris, that great gardener, is a near neighbour, and perhaps I have been influenced unconsciously by his taste for the elusive beauty of species as opposed to the more obvious attractions of hybrids.

Sheltered and with super-perfect drainage, plants of doubtful hardiness such as *Arum creticum* and several *Eucomis* species thrive amongst small protective shrubs of the maquis type in the 'Mediterranean border'. Lilies from Greece, anemones and narcissus from Portugal, iris from Spain, in they all go. I only enrich the dust-like soil here in special cases as these plants are tougher on a starvation diet.

By contrast the north border has quite good soil and here grow the beloved woodlanders. *Helleborus torquatus* underplanted with a raspberry coloured *Hepatica*, drifts of *Anemone nemorosa* 'Alleni'. Hostas large and tiny, arums, arisaemas, *Francoa sonchifolia*, *Kirengeshoma palmata* are all comfortable here.

After about eighteen months I felt equal to tackling the jungle by the stream. Gradually the shape of the gully emerged as a much elongated triangle with the stream tinkling across its base. One of the long sides was a low containing wall and the near side was a steep bank which I discovered was laced with springs. In the middle was an apparently bottomless quagmire.

The shape was unpropitious and inspiration failed me, but finally a visitor suggested having a terrace made under the south wall (on which to meditate in my spare time) and a broad flight of steps down the north facing bank. Then at last began the glorious game of planting up the bank and side of the stream, not to mention the middle. Moisture-loving irises, ligularias and astilbes rioted there, but ultimately I was defeated by sheer physical exhaustion caused by floundering in fathoms of mud and after a few years it was drained and put down to grass.

The terrace bank demands the agility of a goat and I clamber in fear of my life, but get huge pleasure from making mini-groups, tucking in a fern here and there round the logs and flints, or arranging a brilliant patch of *Primula rosea* next to *Hacquetia epipactus* for the early spring. An excellent self-made hybrid primrose sits close to the rare *Salix reticulata* creeping minutely round a log while the bigger *Salix apoda* and *S. myrsinites* glisten with silver catkins further away. Narcissi, trilliums and fountains of *Leucojum aestivum* 'Gravetye Giant' are white amongst the green of veratrums and hostas, and in the autumn *Gentiana asclepiadea* make more spectacular fountains in both blue and white forms, whilst nearby the minute *Gunnera magellanica* holds its red fruits. It is all semi-wild and I mean it to be so; the stream is a wild little sprite of a thing and would hate too much discipline.

Writing this description of my garden has been very salutary and my eyes have shed many scales. I cannot imagine what I have been thinking of not to have done this . . . and that . . . the list is too long. If only I could have the time over again.

Jenny Robinson.

152 The garden near the house. A mosaic of low-growing plants and shrubs includes celmisias, golden marjoram, ballota and a multitude of dwarf bulbs

The Manor House, Cranborne, Dorset

The Marchioness of Salisbury's Garden

I SUPPOSE it is rare to come, through marriage, into a garden that one knew as a child, moreover a garden that had lingered in one's memory as a place of mysterious enchantment and romance. This has been my wonderful good fortune.

I was fourteen when I first saw Cranborne and perhaps I would not have remembered that first glimpse so vividly if I had not been a child-gardener, my eyes having been opened by a present of several packets of annuals and a plot to plant them in. This simple present revealed a veritable Aladdin's cave of delights, a 'paradisi in sole', and created a life-long love of plants and flowers and growing things which was to lead eventually to my work in the garden at Cranborne.

That first view still remains with me, though misty and shadowed. Over the years the picture gradually came into focus, but its sharpness did not change the original vision and the garden for me was always one of mystery and enchantment.

Then in 1954 we came to live at Cranborne. The property had come into my husband's family early in the seventeenth century when it was given to his ancestor, Robert Cecil, by King James I. John Tradescant the Elder was gardener to both Robert Cecil and the King and certainly visited Cranborne, for we have his 'bill of charges on being sent to plant trees there', and we can fairly assume he was responsible for the plans of the garden. I mention something of the history of the garden and Tradescant's connection with it because they have had the greatest influence on my ideas and plantings.

I must confess to having felt a twinge of apprehension at the thought of gardening at Cranborne. I had been used to a small and intimate garden, and although they were of the same date, the Cranborne garden was ten acres larger.

Miss Jekyll said, 'the garden should fit the master and his tastes just as his clothes do; it should be neither too large or too small but just comfortable'. I felt this master was going to be too small for his clothes. Besides was it not already perfect? My mother- and father-in-law were knowledgeable and skilled gardeners and had added many new beauties. Would there be anything left to do in the way of creating, planning and developing which make up so much of the fun of gardening?

All such poor thoughts were soon to vanish in the planning and practical work we had to do if we were to keep the garden going. The labour force was halved, leaving us with four gardeners and a part-timer. We had to decide whether to put a large area back to grass, or to try, by simplification of some of the more elaborate parts, and by more labour-saving planting (less herbaceous and bedding)

116

153 *The church walk at Cranborne, where the double spring borders have a background of apple blossom. The influence is seen of John Tradescant, gardener to Robert Cecil in the 17th century. He too mingled fruit and flowers in his planting*

to retain the whole garden. We decided, thank goodness, to adopt the latter plan. How awful to think of the yew hedges we might have rooted up and happily, thanks mainly to the hard work, skill and expertise of our wonderful team of gardeners, we have not yet had to resort to such measures.

I have already said how much the history of the place and Tradescant's work there influenced my ideas for the planting and planning at Cranborne. His lists of plants and trees led me to read all the Elizabethan and Stuart gardening books I could find, and to visit the beauties of Hidcote and Sissinghurst.

117

*154 Part of the courtyard garden, where mellow
brick walls make a fine background for planting*

*155 Clipped box in the Tudor tradition,
overhung by golden genista*

Knowing the plan of the garden in the seventeenth century and some of the trees and plants grown there, helped to form a picture in my mind's eye of the garden as it may have looked then. The Elizabethan gardens, although in many ways homely and simple, were architectural too, and in a subtle way adhered to the strict rules of form. They were very much extensions of the house they surrounded and with it formed a blended whole, most comfortable to the eye.

This is very true of Cranborne. The walls, attached to the house, surround the courts on the north and south, and the bowling green with its clipped yew allée on its north side forms a green court to the west. The skeleton of Tradescant's garden is still there. The banks he formed to make flat areas for his parterres, the yew hedges at the back of the mount garden, the yew allée and the mount itself, that 'hill made to be clambered up to view a fair prospect'.

I felt, as the Elizabethans and Stuarts had, that I did not want to break with the past. They, simply, had tried to make lovelier all that was most attractive in mediaeval times by 'their principles of beauty and sense of form'. Lacking the mind, outlook, or feelings of those gardeners of long ago one could not, and would not want, to create an exact imitation. However, with the bones of an early plan one could hope perhaps, to regain the feeling and manner of a garden of those times by growing many of the old plants that must have flourished there. The deliciously fragrant homely plants which filled the gardens of the Tudors and Stuarts with sweetness and the hum of bees, fulfilled the idea of a garden as a place where both pleasure and peace were to be found.

So I set to work. The first thing was to try and improve the soil which was poor, thin and chalky over solid chalk, quick draining and easily dried out. Sir Frederic Stern had told us that it was not so much the chalk itself that the plants minded, but not being able to get their roots into it. 'Break it up thoroughly three feet down,' he said. It is important too, not to put the manure and goodies too deep; the roots are better nearer the surface where they get more nourishment and can be fed from above. Drought is a problem, and mulching in the spring is a help.

Our roses were full of blackspot and we used to spray them, but gave up years ago. It took too much precious time and the smell of chemicals in the garden, the smell of death, is not to be abided.

It is said that a healthy body and one full of vitality best resists disease, so the soil must team with life if the plants are to flourish. We poured on loads of leaf mould, peat and manure, and used fish manure, Maxicrop and bonemeal. One year we found some delectable yellow loam on a not too distant farm and piled that on. It had the most dramatic effect on the poor starved plants, and a *Magnolia × highdownensis* which had never grown, shot up like Jack's beanstalk and flowered for the first time.

Along with chemical sprays, weedkillers were banned after several nasty experiences, except for the non-spreaders on the gravel drives, but we do use the non-poisonous insecticides like derris and pyrethrum, and a herbal slug killer.

I had always loved the old fashioned flowers best with their delicious scents and restful charm, qualities not often found in modern hybrids or compensated for by size and colour. My mother-in-law had collected old and species roses and I set about adding to the collection and we propagated many under mist to get them on their own roots. With Tradescant's lists and my mind full of the Tudor and Stuart gardens I planted his 'great white roses', the albas, along with damasks, gallicas and centifolias. Herbs went into the beds and borders, hyssop, savory and thyme, pinks, violas and cistus – Tradescant's Holyrose – taking the place of bedding out and herbaceous plants along with under

156 The Manor House approached through the Elizabethan gatehouse. The meadow grass in the foreground is mown only at intervals that are carefully timed to encourage wild flowers

157 The knot garden is filled entirely with plants that were grown in 16th and 17th century gardens. The statue of St. Rocco presides over the scene

plantings of spring and autumn bulbs. Under the crab apples in the orchard I planted quantities of autumn crocus, prompted by a memory of meadows in France where the pale goblets of 'the little naked boys' grow in the close scythed grass of the orchards.

I planted thickly to clothe the ground, and to have greys and greens and the blue of rue in winter time and to nudge out the weeds, edging the beds in the herb garden with lavender cotton and the knot garden with box. Auriculas were added, *Alchemilla* and double primroses, columbines and striped tulips and for the most part they settled in happily and seemed to be as harmonious as a woman's face in the right hat.

I have had a lot of fun with the knot garden. Here I have been a purist and grown only plants used in the sixteenth and seventeenth centuries. Friends, generous and kind, have given me ancient pinks, rose plantain, the double sweet rocket and gold laced polyanthus, and they grow with Gerard's double primrose, and plumed and double hyacinths and the stately Crown Imperial without which no early knot was complete.

At the head of the knot stands a seventeenth-century statue of St. Rocco. We found him in Italy, staff in hand, with his scallop shell on his shoulder. As one looks at his beneficent face, Robert de la Condamines' words come into one's mind. 'The saint has come out into the garden from his little cell, he has come out into the evening air to look upon the roses. One walks with him and the ministry of angels is with him.' In winter we wrap him in a snug coat of bracken and hessian against the destroying frosts.

Much wished for was a white garden, and we made one in the North Court with a scattering of buffs and apricots to emphasize the whites. In the old kitchen garden I tried to create what to George Eliot was the ideal garden, her description of it had charmed me. She praised a garden full of homely plants, vegetables and fruit (Tradescant too had mingled fruit and flowers) as, 'a charming para-

120

158 *The herb garden, enclosed by walls and clipped yews. The small beds are edged with low santolina, and four standard honeysuckles surround the circular stone urn*

disiacal mingling of all that was pleasant to the eyes and good for food. . . . You gathered a moss-rose one moment and a bunch of currants the next; you were in a delicious fluctuation between the scent of jasmine and the juice of gooseberries; the crimson of a carnation was carried out in the lurking of the neighbouring strawberry beds.' But we had our troubles.

The apple hedges would not grow. In despair I asked a man who knew all about apples, to help us. We simply had the wrong kinds for our miserable soil, and he sent me some old fashioned varieties that tolerate it and now flourish. The bindweed too was a menace till a kind friend told us about the bucket of weak MCPA into which you put your hands, covered in woollen gloves, on top of rubber ones, which you then smear on the weed. I broke my ban and tried this too with the Bishops weed (surely an unfrocked priest) which had been tiresome and walked into the box hedges in the mount garden, but with only partial success.

'A weed is a plant in the wrong place,' my great uncle-in-law used to say. He was eighty, and fond of repeating this truism whenever I stopped in our slow perambulations, to pull out a trespasser. I enjoy showing friends and sometimes strangers round, especially gardeners, when I get a rare chance to take a more objective view of the garden.

Marjorie Salisbury

121

The late Mrs Patrick Saunders's Garden

FINDING FLOWERS in their native haunts has always been the greatest thrill of my life and Gerard's *Herbal* has been my bible. I met John Codrington, the garden designer, on a botanical expedition in 1951 and he has helped me with plants and advice ever since. When I arrived here in 1950 the garden was in perfect order, very formal and tidy; it didn't appeal to me at all. Strong nephews removed yards of crazy paving, underneath were a host of daffodils. Fastigiate cypresses were dug from the corners of herbaceous borders and given away. Following John Codrington's advice I enlarged the pond and gave it a natural look with a background of the pretty, small-leafed bamboo *Arundinaria nitida*, purple hazels, *Rubus* × 'Tridel' and *Rosa* 'Buff Beauty'.

Ever since those early days I have been fascinated with trying to grow the plants I have seen in their native surroundings. I have violets from France, Australia and America, hellebores from Rumania and Italy, snowdrops from Greece and Turkey, tulips from Afghanistan and Persia, primroses,

159 and 160 *Hellebores at Orchard Cottage, which is a garden for specialists. Mrs Saunders collected many plants from abroad. (Left)* Galanthus nivalis *and* Helleborus orientalis. *(Right)* Helleborus bocconei *from Italy*

122

Daphne and *Bergenia* from Nepal and wild roses from America. The families that interest me most are snowdrops, cyclamen and hellebores, perhaps because they can be studied in the winter, when there is more time.

The whole area is just one acre, consisting of an old orchard, the garden round the cottage and a kitchen garden at the back. In the spring the scent of the balsam poplar's buds fills the garden and in summer the sweet smell of the weeping silver lime. The tall shrub *Daphne bholua*, which I collected in Nepal as a seedling in 1970, is the sweetest daphne of all this wonderfully fragrant family, and *Rosa helenae* climbs a perry pear tree and scents the garden in July. My favourite fragrant shrub is

161 The main border near the house in this richly-stocked limestone garden. Every plant has an association and is carefully given its appropriate conditions. Elsewhere in the garden is a lime-free bed for pieris, Camellia × williamsii 'Donation', Daphne bholua, *trilliums and auratum lilies*

162 *A collection of special plants.* (Top, left to right) *(a)* Helleborus multifidus serbicus (dumetorum) *from Rumania, (b)* H. purpurescens *from Rumania (c)* Galanthus 'S. Arnott'. (Bottom) *(d)* Daphne bholua, *a seedling collected from Nepal in 1970, (e)* Petasites japonicus *in flower, later its huge leaves emerge, (f)* Leucojum vernum carpaticum

Rhododendron decorum, which is lime tolerant, provided it is planted with plenty of peat and leaf mould. The white bell-shaped blooms smell heavenly in May.

My aim is to make the collected wild flowers adapt to their new home and multiply. As I grow older and increasingly deaf I enjoy my hours in the garden more than ever before. Growing plants is a never-failing source of delight, and this must be so if a garden is to fulfil the search for happiness.

Nancy Saunders

A FEW PLANTS COLLECTED FROM ABROAD

Elephant's ears	*Bergenia ciliata*	Nepal
Lenten roses	*Helleborus purpurascens H. dumetorum*	Rumania
	H. bocconei H. viridis orientalis and 29 other varieties	Calabria, Italy
Primroses	*Primula vulgaris sibthorpii*	Persia
	P. petiolaris	Nepal
Roses	*Rosa foliolosa R. nitida*	U.S.A.
	R. ecae	Afghanistan
Snowdrops	*Galanthus byzantinus* and 43 other varieties	Turkey
Spindle	*Euonymus cornutus quinquecornutus*	China
Willow	*Salix bockii* and 22 other varieties	China

The Dower House, Badminton, Avon

The Lady Caroline Somerset's Garden

ONE OF the many tediums of life is the fact that it is rare for anyone to take a real interest in gardening until they have reached early middle age. If only one could get over all those kindergarten mistakes in one's youth, then one would be able to enjoy a mature garden for the rest of one's life. However, like most people I was thirty-five before I acquired a garden. Up to this point I had always loved to wander round other people's gardens saying, 'Oh how pretty' and 'Doesn't that rose smell nice?' and other such fatuous remarks. I never inquired about names and I remember someone once saying, 'Now that is Kiftsgate,' and I said, 'Oh really, I thought it was lavender'. So when I took over my three acre garden my ignorance was of the deepest variety. I did not realize it at the time but I was extremely lucky, because although my garden had been totally let go and was a sea of bindweed and ground elder, it had 'bones'. These consisted of a huge yew hedge, at least one hundred and fifty years old, walls, an orchard and a couple of good sized trees. The lawn was adequate, but only just, and I have never ceased to regret that I did not plough it up and reseed it that first year. Of course I could still do so now, but it's unlikely that I will bring myself to do it.

　With the confidence of a total beginner I set about planning where the new yew hedges should go. I had always admired and knew that I wanted the same type of garden as my mother-in-law, Betty Somerset had, different rooms leading one into the other; enclosures filled with

163 Rose 'Raubritter'. This rose cascades over a low wall on the terrace beside the house

164 Part of the immensely old yew hedges. They are a great feature and provide a natural structure for this beautiful garden. Here they create a background for a close planting of shrub roses and ground cover

old fashioned roses and a mass of different grey foliage. This may not be very original, but it is what I like.

I did my first garden shopping, which consisted of ten washing lines. These I laid out over the lawn. I then sat down in this maze of ropes and spent a very happy hour visualizing them as yew hedges and overflowing flower beds. More by luck than good judgement I got the proportions more or less right although Russell Page, at a later date, did have to square them up somewhat.

I next engaged a gardener, Mr Bryan, a most charming man who had been the home farm cowman and who had never done any gardening except in his own allotment. He got rid of the ground elder with one good digging. The bindweed took at least three years and still presents a problem. Much as I loathe the stuff I do derive immense satisfaction everytime I ease out several feet of that white root.

I bought a gardening encyclopaedia, which Mr Bryan and I spent hours pondering over. We got the yew hedges in and immediately I felt the pride of creation. I started ordering the plants for the borders with enthusiasm. My first order was pathetic in its ignorance. 'Twelve pink paeonies, daffodils, furry lambs ears, lilies and mauve lilac', no mention of which type I wanted. I did not even know that there were different types. Luckily for me the nursery sent some very pretty varieties and so Mr Bryan and I began planting. I made the usual beginner's mistakes. I planted things too close together and in too small groups. After fifteen years of gardening I am afraid that I am still making the same mistakes.

The first spring it seemed a miracle that things which had been planted were actually growing. It

126

165 *The folly in the vegetable garden. Standard 'Iceberg' roses line the brick path. In midsummer the folly is so smothered with roses, clematis, solanum and jasmine that it succeeds in 'looking like one of Queen Mary's prettiest toques'*

166 A model herb garden, decoratively and conveniently planned near the kitchen

167 Box-edged beds filled with old-fashioned roses, in the secret garden

was then that the seeds were sown in me to become the gardening bore that I now am. However there was one slight bone of discontent which, looking back, I really rather enjoyed complaining about. My husband was not particularly interested in the garden. 'Such a pity', I used to say in a martyrish way. I was wrong. Now, not only is he extremely interested but we fight like fury over what we are going to do. We have basic differences. He wishes to have effect. If he likes something he says, 'Order a lot more'. Whereas I am more of a collector and get immense pleasure from some dingy little plant just because it is rare or difficult to grow. Then in the pond garden, he wants the yew hedges to be seven feet tall and to walk behind them into a secret garden. I think that the area is too small for this and want them to be a mere four feet so that one can see the roses over the top. If ever we get divorced, it won't be for adultery, or any misdemeanour like that, it will be for a major sin, such as him pulling out my euphorbias or me cutting the tops of those hedges. The irritating thing is that he is usually right. But not always! Now I look back on the good old days when I was not being interfered with and was foolish enough to grizzle about it.

In those early days I was even more obsessed with the garden than I am now. I bought endless books, and memorized hundreds of names. Latin came into my life, to a point of snobbism. I never called a yew a yew I called it taxus, I have no difficulty in learning names but to retain them in my head from one year to another proves to be almost an impossibility. If, in the first year, I fail to label the plant, it remains anonymous until some kind person can tell me what it is. My dog is no help to me. He pulls out any label stuck in the ground and has lately taken to pulling out the plants themselves. Then some of the visitors who come round the garden appear to collect labels like other people collect stamps. If ever I catch them pocketing one I shall display an unreasonable amount of temper. It is a deep humiliation to me to be asked for a name and to have to confess that I do not know it.

Mr Bryan's green fingers were most necessary in the next few years because I played incessant musical chairs with everything. One wretched rose bush moved four times in four years and survived. Fortunately for us Russell Page came into our lives, just too late to put us right over the swimming pool but not too late to help me with the yellow, silver and white border beside it, which is a success.

Together – David and I arguing – Russell as the expert arbitrator, we turned our attention to the kitchen garden. We laid brick paths with box edging either side. Everyone said that we were mad to plant box, that it would be a lot of work. It is. My present gardener spends three back-breaking days every year, and I know that if I had to cut it myself it would be pulled out in a trice. When I was about to plant it I was told that everyone was getting rid of their edging, so I could certainly get it for nothing. Could I find anyone that was doing so? Everyone had just done it. 'What a pity, we burnt it all.' So I had to buy a hundred yards of it at hideous expense which I resented. Either side of the paths we have narrow borders reserved for bedding out, which are filled with tulips in spring, and a variety of plants in summer. Again everyone goes on about bedding out being such hard work. However, in this case it appears to get done in one day. But once again I must admit it is not me who does it. Behind the borders there are espalier apple trees and behind them gloriously regimented rows of vegetables.

In late summer the kitchen garden is the only area I like. The main part of the garden is short-lived in its full beauty, and by the end of July all the beds have an untidy, hairy look. It is then that the military kitchen garden is fully appreciated. Russell Page designed a very pretty folly for the centre. When it was first put up, I was desperate to get it well covered, so bought the most rampant roses, clematis, solanums and jasmines and waited impatiently. I now regret this hasty buying as it rapidly became far too crowded. However at one point it does succeed in looking like one of the prettiest of Queen Mary's toques.

168 Looking across the terrace from the sitting-room in summer. A combination of formal and exuberant planting creates year-long interest

169 *The 'Potager' where a combination of flowers and vegetables creates a French ambience unusual in England. In the background is a large bush of* Hebe salicifolia

Russell Page has been most patient with me. I am frequently pig-headed and am apt to insist on doing what I want. It usually does not take me more than a year to find out that what I have done is wrong and that what he advised was right. He is then very tactful. He never says, 'I told you so,' but merely, 'I'm glad to see you have changed that.'

Mr Bryan, aged seventy-six, now only comes for half the week, but I am lucky enough to have another delightful man full time, Mr Bailey. So when people ask how many gardeners I have I tell them, 'one and a half'. 'How do they manage?' they ask, adding, 'But of course you must do a lot of work yourself.' 'Well yes, naturally,' I reply complacently and then find myself looking furtively round to see if Mr Bailey or Mr Bryan can hear me. Because, in all honesty, I do precious little. I like pruning, do a bit of weeding, love dead heading (most therapeutic) and even do a bit of mulching. My husband does even less than I do, so I still have something to complain about, though once again I had better take care because he does occasionally 'prune' something. He does not believe in cutting back to the second shoot, in fact he does not even believe in secateurs but attacks the wretched bush with shears and an axe. I scream with anguish but have to admit that so far whatever he has assaulted has thrived.

One of the things that keeps me enthusiastic is competition. I go round other people's gardens with a jealous eye. I see someone's roses growing without a touch of blackspot (one of my many banes) and feel sick with envy. What makes me a really happy woman is to go round some garden which I think is wrongly constructed, planted in bad taste and rather untidy. I am then extraordinarily civil to the owner, say how beautiful everything is and go home in a highly contented frame of mind. I am not a nice character.

I suppose that the charm of gardening is the uncertainty. Even the skilled person has occasional failures. Mine have been legion. But the joy of the successes compensates. Last June, David and I were walking round the garden one evening (early morning and late evening are always the most beautiful moments) and we looked at each other and said, 'You know, it really is very pretty'. It was a rare moment of satisfaction and two huge, smug smiles spread over our happy faces.

But let not the sobering thought be forgotten, that it is easy, if you have a modicum of taste to create a pretty garden, but it is damn difficult to keep it going.

Caroline Somerset

Coates Manor, Fittleworth, Sussex

Mrs Gilbert Thorp's Garden

WHEN MY husband and I came to Coates Manor in 1960 we had chosen the house and not the garden. The house had been derelict, the land around wild and neglected and neither of us were then gardeners. The house, a scheduled, stone-built, small Elizabethan manor, looked gaunt and unloved and I realized that it needed an appropriate setting.

I knew the type of garden which would satisfy me as I had spent many years flower arranging, and had developed a preference for interesting foliage; I never wanted a blaze of colour. Also the garden had to be planned for me to maintain single-handed, or with very little extra help, and for this reason I have no greenhouse. It is surprising what can be done in the garden with cuttings under jam jars.

I read the books of Michael Haworth-Booth which appealed to me and I visited his garden. He chose his flowering trees and shrubs demanding not only one or two weeks of glorious blossom but also berries, interesting foliage and autumn colour. In my case, with only an acre of land, this discrimination in the choice of plants was essential.

During our first summer we studied the garden from every aspect: the sun and how it affected different corners from early morning to late evening, the wind and where it would be necessary to provide shelter, the frost and where it lay longest.

170 In the main garden behind the house at Coates Manor. Betula pendula dalecarlica *is underplanted with* Artemisia absinthium 'Lambrook Silver', *and massed agapanthus*

171 A standard wisteria with a group of Helleborus orientalis *at its feet. The archway is covered by* Clematis montana rubens *and a golden leafed euonymus*

172 *A sea of blue agapanthus. Features in the distance are a juniper and a catalpa*

173 *In the walled garden. Junipers contrast with a fastigiate golden yew*

One of the first jobs was to remove two feet of brick paving from the foot of the house to provide planting space on either side of the front door. We cleared away the accumulation of the ages and dug a border six feet wide round our front boundary to secure our privacy. In later years this has been shaped to give wider and narrower planting. The soil was well mulched with farmyard manure. During our first autumn Mr. Haworth-Booth provided a skeleton planting for this border, not all of which has survived.

At about this time, I was introduced to Jackman's Nurseries of Woking and to Arthur Tomes who was then in charge of their stock ground. His influence on the choice of good varieties of species shows up in the garden today. His knowledge came from a life of gardening experience which he shared generously with those anxious to learn. He taught me patience to wait for a good plant to mature, to prune, an essential art often overlooked, and the necessity to keep the soil in good heart by feeding. He was my tutor and I had to learn the Latin names of plants and their correct spelling.

Today, the front border is a blend of coloured foliage, purple-red, grey and gold. There is copper beech and the purple leafed form of the 'Smoke tree'; for grey I have included sea buckthorn and weeping pear, and for gold *Elaeagnus pungens* 'Maculata' and golden yew. The under-planting is golden grass, blue rue, and 'lambs ear'. Day lilies give flower colour and contrast of leaf shape along with the clean line of *Bergenia cordifolia*.

The design of the garden evolved as I worked gradually from front to back. At the same time I was reading the books of Gertrude Jekyll, E. A. Bowles, Canon Ellacombe, William Robinson and Vita Sackville-West, together with those by Russell Page and Christopher Lloyd, and learning what to try and achieve. I was, and still am, always searching for good plant associations and am in no way a compulsive collector of plants. Here, flower arranging has had an influence and I think this shows in the garden planting. I have no inhibitions over variegated foliage plants and a greater appreciation of them has been brought about by the National Association of Flower Arrangement Societies.

A successful colour theme I have used has mainly blues and yellows, the free flowering 'Mount Etna

132

Broom' and a golden *Catalpa* underplanted with a lovely blue spruce and hardy *Agapanthus*. Again, influenced by my flower arranging, I have made a combination of horizontal lines using the swallow shaped *Prunus* 'Tsubame' and *Juniperus* × *media* 'Pfitzeriana Aurea'.

Choosing the right specimen trees is most important. We decided to have a walnut for the front lawn because it was introduced into this country about the time the house was built. In another part of the garden we planted a birch with pure white trunk and branches for its beauty, which has been given a carpet of the Canary Island ivy and the combination is lovely throughout the year. A single specimen *Liquidamber styraciflua* 'Worplesden' planted in the lawn gives vivid autumn colour. Conifers are used to give permanent interest throughout the year and to create architectural effects.

Only plants that respond to our local conditions are grown, and at times it is necessary to be ruthless. Late spring frosts play havoc with trees and shrubs which come into leaf early and because of this many choice plants have been lost. I have always ordered and planted in the late autumn and have not resorted to container grown plants, mainly because these need extra care and attention, especially in a garden which quickly dries out in hot weather.

Surprise is achieved by a small walled garden leading from the open lawn at the back of the house. This with its central path provides wall space and enables low growing plants to spill over onto the path thereby breaking the hard lines. As it is over-looked by the house it has to provide year round interest. On the walls grow *Ceanothus* 'Henri Desfosse', *C.* 'Edinburgh', variegated jasmine, *Clematis* 'Perle d'Azur', *Vitis vinifera* 'Purpurea' and scented honeysuckles. There is scent again in the borders with *Choisya ternata*, *Philadelphus coronarius* 'Variegatus' with lilies growing through them.

Inevitably, a garden never stands still and requires the care, over one or two generations, of people with similar ideas, to mature and develop in complete balance. It is necessary to be alone in the garden to stand and look and think quietly and have ideas. The best time to enjoy any garden is in the early morning or late evening when all is quiet. This is not, alas, the time when most gardens are open to the public.

Margaret Thorp

174 *Looking through the archway to a beautiful specimen* Liquidambar styraciflua *'Worplesden', framed with golden variegated ivy and a purple-leafed cotinus*

175 *The same Liquidambar seen across the lawn. Beyond it are the golden catalpa, and a bush of silver-leafed privet*

Shute House, Donhead St Mary, Dorset

The Lady Anne Tree's Garden

OUR GARDEN existed, and indeed was deeply cared for by the previous owner, but unfortunately he had not been able to maintain it fully. Apart from the area around the house it was overgrown and shapeless, but the site itself was marvellous, a garden, with many springs and ponds, the source of a river, with its ration of mature trees. It faces south overlooking farmland and distant downs that gently slope into the surrounding countryside.

Our immediate reaction was that we must have an overall plan, correctly scaled and architected, and to this end we asked Geoffrey Jellicoe to create us something to which we could all contribute. Geoffrey and my husband worked on the plan together. I asked for specific ideas to be included, and it was agreed the planting was to be mine. Mr Jellicoe is a joy to work with and a great expert on garden creation. Failure does not exist in his mind, only solutions; his imagination is fertile and subtle. My husband has thoroughness and imagination.

Our first problem was clearing and dredging. All the water except the source of the Nadder was invisible. Aged *Rhododendron ponticum* and thick bamboo hid the shape of the ponds and streams. The water itself was silted up and needed draining before we could get rid of the mud. The site began to look more and more like photographs of the battle of Mons and the clearing took over a year. By the time the ponticum were removed and the ponds cleared we were, except for the area of lawn round the house, starting from scratch. But the plan was ready and we set to work to create our three acre garden on greensand soil.

Geoffrey Jellicoe gave us a wonderful layout. He designed a water garden cascading down a hill. In the cascades are copper mouldings designed to produce a musical chord as the water tumbles over them. The water is banked on either side by asymmetrical beds, abstract in shape at ground level and backed by beech hedges. The water is bridged by wide flag-stones which run into garden paths, leading through the beech hedge into different walks about the garden.

Apart from the master plan I did not ask for advice; in fact in the early stages of planting a garden I can't bear advice. It interrupts my train of thought and I would feel as though someone was painting my picture for me. For me planting is an ego trip and I like to indulge myself to the full.

Obviously colour is of prime consideration. I try to follow the dominant colours of the wild flowers of the season. Every season has its own light and the tones of the wild flowers suit this light. Thus, in the spring I love plenty of pale yellow; in the summer a riot of colour; and in the autumn misty tones. Winter flowers are my special favourites, particularly species bulbs.

134

176 *The water garden at Shute House. The water tumbling over copper mouldings produces a musical effect. The symmetrical beds beside the water are filled with a lush planting, as shown in this spring scene. The water is bridged by wide flagstones which lead into various garden walks*

177 *One of many fine examples of* Cynara cardunculus *near the water garden. Great use is made of many forms of silver plants and ornamental pots*

In planting, shading and silhouette are all-important. I shade with a pale or darker tone of the same colour, mauve with purple, pink with red, pale yellow with dark yellow, pale and dark blue. I never shade with white as it divides one colour from another too harshly and breaks up the over-all effect. White alone is beautiful, or if used with silver, or best of all with mixed greens. Never forget silhouette: giant thistles, artichokes, topiary make a skyline. By the water garden I have a fine plantation of cardoons and scotch thistle. They last for two months and look beautiful in all weathers. Further down, near an eighteen foot gazebo and overlooking a small waterfall, I have planted a group of white poplars behind a bank of laurel and yew. This is for the future, but has the bones of a successful group.

As for scent you cannot have enough of it. Tobacco, phlox, rose, box, sweet geranium, lilies, orange blossom, honeysuckle – the list is endless and a source of unending joy. I use scented plants round the house, against the walls and in tubs so that in summer there is always the scent coming through the open windows.

Herb gardens bore me, I can't bear modern roses, and I dislike the trend of enlarging flowers that are already large enough. This is usually done at the expense of their smell, or making a stem so big and brittle it breaks in the first summer storm.

I have no favourite season. Change seems to come at exactly the right psychological moment. I try to have as many different seasonal plants as possible, so that the garden is botanically interesting, as well as satisfactory in form and scale.

I suppose the gardens of my childhood have influenced me as I am still fascinated by an atmosphere of mystery. As a child I was intrigued by a secret world of large plants and rocks and splashing water, cold in reality, but in essence like the tropics; a garden in which I could get lost and make a new discovery on almost every outing. Later visits to Italian gardens affected me with an emotion that amounted to shock. The Italian use of water, their skill with shade, and on a humbler level, the decorative effect of pots of every shape and size, from those used in the grandest courtyard to the lowliest back yard.

As I get older I like to gaze at the natural landscape and I feel that a garden should be a part of its surroundings. I would prefer that my garden should not be laid out like a map, and a visitor realize he is in a man-made creation only when he walks round the garden.

Visits to R.H.S. shows are essential, a positive blood transfusion which alleviates ignorance and frequently introduces a beautiful new plant to my life. Occasional bouts of insomnia are helpful too. I ponder for hours on a problem in the garden and before sleep comes, with luck, the problem solves itself. I wake with a sense of anticipation.

We grow a great many flowers and vegetables from seed, and take cuttings of geraniums and other treasures, although we do not have the labour, heat, or space in which to propagate.

It is difficult to say what successful plantings one has made. So much is in the mind's eye. I'm pleased with a topiary bedroom I have planted. It consists of a four-poster bed, the bed and bolster of box, the curtains a canopy of vines. In a good year the vine crops and grapes hang down. There is a large armchair of sweetbriar which we cut back, leaving the flowering buds to make a natural chintz. The bedside table is of flowing variegated ivy. Last and least successful is the dressing table of yew. Later, when we are less busy, I am going to have a patterned carpet of purple and golden thyme.

Mistakes are too many to list, particularly as I find planting too close together hard to resist. The plant cannot develop and justice is not done to an object of beauty. The fault comes from impatience and the longing for a quick effect.

Often, too, I try a plant that does not like the soil or situation. I am disappointed at the result, but perhaps because I am ardently anti-capital punishment and a Christian pantheist, I find it difficult to consign the offending plant to the bonfire.

We use a lot of well rotted manure on the beds and blood and bone meal on the hedges. We also foliar-feed the camellias and hedges every two weeks throughout the summer with startling effect. We use propachlor to prevent annual weeds growing at the base of the hedges, after they have been hoed in the spring, and again in midsummer. This saves an enormous amount of tedious labour.

178 The topiary bedroom. The four-poster bed is formed from clipped box, the curtains are a canopy of vines. The armchair is of sweetbriar with a natural chintz of pink buds. A carpet of purple and golden thyme is planned

*179 The waterfall into the lake, which reflects
the background of pale* Rhododendron ponticum

*180 The bog garden, where ferns, foxgloves,
primulas and meconopsis are naturalized*

We are lucky to have a full-time gardener in Mr William Taylor, who was a gardener at Sissinghurst
for all his working life until Vita Sackville-West died. He has great experience and knowledge. We
also have Mr Grey, an old age pensioner who works for us three times a week, and for whom nothing
seems impossible. My husband does an incredible amount of weeding and edging and keeps everything tidy. He is also a fund of ideas.

Showing people the garden can be a pleasure, but basically it is a place to be in alone. I would hate
the garden to be open except on odd days for charity. I like gardening alone and the feeling that the
garden is empty.

A garden changes constantly. Empty spaces appear where casualties occur. Clearing becomes
necessary to allow shrubs and trees to grow. One must keep an open mind. Nothing is more gratifying
than to find a space, search the garden for a refill from an overcrowded spot, transplant the refill
within minutes and wait anxiously till the next morning, and see the subject perky and upright.

Garden centres are another joy; they open a world of possibilities. I choose my specimens with care,
drive home and plant them there and then. I go out after dinner in the summer and imagine how my
plants will look when fully grown. It is the same kind of satisfaction as anticipating a good meal.

I have no favourite part of the garden. It depends on the season, on the day, on the light, whether it is
hot or cold, or whether there is an east wind or a gentle breeze.

My aim in the garden is to provide an area that is beautiful under some condition on every day of the
year. Of course I fail, but the interest never flags, and the challenge provides a constant stimulus.
A shrub flowers for the first time, or an apparently dead creeper revives and I am content.

Anne Tree

Barnsley House, Cirencester, Gloucestershire

Mrs David Verey's Garden

THE RIGHT set of circumstances arising at just the right moment – as in many of one's major experiences – profoundly influenced my life, and turned me into a gardener absorbed by the craft, its history and the art it can become. When we came to live here in 1951 there was no time for gardening. The family were young and needed all my energies. After ten years my husband firmly suggested that I should try to take the garden in hand. He reminded me that I had grassed over most of his parents' borders to make wide open spaces for cricket, croquet and even ponies, always promising that one day the plants would be reinstated. Suddenly that day had come.

The garden already had many marvellous features – a beautiful house built in 1697 of honey-coloured Cotswold stone, surrounding walls ending in an amusing Gothic alcove, trees more than one hundred years old, yew hedges and yards of box planted in the nineteenth century; enough to make any gardener of experience and judgement jealous. Perhaps best of all was the soil which in places had been cultivated for generations. The assurance that people had lived and gardened here for so long was a tremendous incentive for me to add my contribution. But, curiously, I knew I need not

hurry, and I still have this feeling. Good 'bones' are important, so it is wise to go slowly and get your plan right before launching into a vital project. Now I love thinking out and creating a new incident. Then I felt totally bewildered and unable to start.

How does one begin? In retrospect the important events seem incidental and fortuitous. As a 1960 Christmas present our eldest son gave me a subscription to the R.H.S. and our youngest daughter a large empty notebook labelled 'Your Gardening Book'. The vital impetus has always been my husband urging me on, expecting new

181 Golden aconites make a solid carpet in February under the plane trees, chestnuts and limes which border the drive. Snowdrops, crocus, scillas, hellebores and daffodils follow nearby

borders to be made in a flash and imagining I would know how to do it. He laid a path with large pebbles picked up on the beaches in south Wales and planted the start of our lime walk. He had a lily pond made which later turned out to be the exact width of the classical 'temple' he was given and then had moved, stone by stone, from Fairford Park. He gave me Russell Page's *Education of a Gardener* and books by Vita Sackville-West. Between them all they made me determined to try to create something beautiful.

I became a compulsive visitor to the 'fortnightly' shows at Vincent Square and there found a wealth of gardening inspiration awaiting me. The early spring and autumn shows are still my favourites. Those first bulbs with their amazing delicacy are a recurrent miracle. Iris, crocus, anemones with their subtle clear colours are a delight to examine at close quarters, then to select for one's own garden. At my first autumn show though, I was bowled over by the beauty of the massed array of autumn colour. Obviously I had been living with my eyes half closed. But I soon discovered that many of the trees which turn brilliant autumn shades do not like our limestone soil. Gazing in admiration at *Sorbus* 'Embley' and *Vitis coignetiae* I asked the owner of the stand, rather tentatively, if either would thrive on our Cotswold limestone. To my delight he said they both would. Later I called at the nursery, Sherrard's of Newbury, and together we planned the first plantings of what we now call 'the wilderness'. I will always be grateful to Tim Sherrard for patiently helping me, for his advice and enthusiasm. We put in a number of long-term trees, a cedar, a tulip tree, catalpa, a wellingtonia, two metasequoias and a ginkgo. For spring there are flowering cherries and crabs. The most beautiful now in blossom are *Prunus* 'Ukon' and *P.* 'Tai Haku'. In autumn *Malus tschonoskii*, turns a fiery red. The whitebeams, *Sorbus aria* 'Lutescens' and *S.* 'Mitchellii' are remarkable in May when their grey leaf buds unfurl, and for autumn colour *S.* 'Embley' and *S. sargentiana* are outstanding.

A start had been made, which was a great relief, but still the main flower garden near the house had no plan. Luckily at this point – still 1962 – Russell Page's book was published. I was fascinated by his originality and certain important messages came through to me. There must be a starting point for a

182 The knot garden. A rosemary hedge surrounds two early knot designs. The interlacing threads are made of different box varieties and Teucrium chamaedrys *(wall germander)*

183 The herb garden. Dwarf box hedges make compartments of diamonds and triangles for each individual herb. The wall is covered by a huge Rosa longicuspis
184 (Right) Looking along the broad border towards the temple. In the foreground are Olearia × scilloniensis, Gleditschia triacanthos *'Sunburst' and* Polemonium caeruleum

composition, and use must be made of the longest distances to create vistas, to lead the eye on and on. Each area of the garden must merge smoothly into the next, each have different moods and areas of light and shade. The garden must be designed to look inviting even in winter, when evergreens and shapes assume importance. Sweet smelling winter flowering shrubs should be near the house. An element of surprise is essential, and I must never forget that simplicity is often best. As for plants I must get to know them, so I can choose them to suit their sites as well as their neighbours.

My gardening notebook (now in volume IV) became a rag-bag of thoughts. There were names of trees and plants, new to me then and often entered three or four times before I finally recognized them. Visits to famous gardens and especially striking plant associations were noted. I saw mounds of purple sage with dark red tulips in one garden and with velvet-red Tuscany roses in another, apple green hart's tongue ferns between grey hostas. Those circular pools of grey and gold carpeting under old apple trees at Powis Castle, rue and golden marjoram, lamium and creeping jenny – one day they would be adopted in our garden.

I had to be practical, so following Russell Page's advice I got down to pencil and squared paper and attempted to make elementary plans. My starting point was the drawing-room door, leading on to an existing Cotswold stone path flanked with Irish yews, which had been planted in 1948. I sowed rock rose seed between the paving and now, years later they have taken over the path and become a controversial feature. I drew my border shapes round this path, four of them, as symmetrically as possible. The shapes were correct but the planting was hopeless. Nancy Lindsay came to my rescue

141

185 *The terrace after rain*. Alchemilla mollis *has spread through the paving stones*

with her good hellebores, hardy geraniums, euphorbias and plenty of advice. She gave me three mandrakes, which was another fortuitous event.

My husband was left several architectural books and amongst them was a paper on *The Insane Root*, in fact the mandrake. I read that Hippocrates advised 'administer less of the drug than causes madness', and Pliny said it would induce sleep, and the Romans used it as an anaesthetic. Every writer on herbs from BC until the eighteenth century mentions this mysterious mandrake and the deadly danger of being within earshot of its screams as it is pulled up. What intrigued me was, who were these early writers and how could I find their herbals? I wanted to know more about William Turner, garden adviser to the Duke of Somerset, Lord Protector to young Edward VI, who published his herbal in 1551, and about Gerard and Parkinson. With beginner's good fortune at the first book sale that I went to there was a periodical article bound as a book *The Herbal in Antiquity* by Charles Singer and another book *The Woad Plant and its Dye* by Dr. Jamieson Hurry. They were the start of my book collecting which opened an entirely new approach to gardens.

I was fascinated by the early knot garden designs and the later grand formal layouts influenced by the French. Scholarly books have been written on the history of garden design, but people wanting to reconstruct old gardens historically and understand their meaning should read the contemporary books as well. In the sixteenth and seventeenth centuries the design was of tremendous importance for there were many less plants to use, in fact formality and design were essential. Borders as we think of them only came about with the availability and introduction of plant material. Reading the old books and visiting great gardens made my head swim with ambitious thoughts of combining formality with luxuriance of planting, always trying to remember that every added detail should be a contribution not a distraction.

The lime walk was extended into an arched laburnum avenue to create a longer vista. We opened up the view from the temple, again to make it as long as possible, and Simon Verity, a local sculptor, made us a fountain for a focal point. The area of ornamental trees was re-named 'the wilderness' and paths were mown to give it an eighteenth century touch. I attempted to make a knot garden and a patterned herb garden. Clipping the box 'threads' takes a long time, but the result is rewarding.

Another landmark was reading in a Victorian book that in order to keep your garden full you must always be propagating, so we set up a small mist propagator. That was in 1964 and since then we must have created thousands of plants. This has been the greatest help, for it is marvellous to be able to go to the greenhouse yard with a large wheelbarrow and choose from an abundance of plants. Now I positively look forward to finding a gap in a border which I can refill with some choice treasure.

I can think of many incidents and places which have influenced me. After seeing the golden border at Pyrford Court, made by Gertrude Jekyll, I was determined to use the same theme, and now ours really glows in the sunlight and creates its own light on dull days. The restfulness of sitting in an enclosed and paved compartment in Sir Gordon Russell's garden filled me with longing and we have now paved our pond garden with Cotswold stones, keeping selected trees and shrubs as features. To emphasize the change from grass to paving we added Georgian wrought iron gates and railings. All this has produced a more peaceful atmosphere.

New projects are always exciting and our latest has been trying to make the vegetable garden more interesting. We have laid it out with old brick and block paths, adapting the designs from William Lawson's *Country Housewife's Garden*. His advice was never to have your beds more than five feet wide so the 'weeder women' need not tread on them. We have found this very good counsel. Four apple trees are being trained as goblets and others as single tier espaliers. Both of these thoughts are derived from De La Quintinye's fruit garden at Versailles where he was in charge of Louis XIV's potager and had to provide the Sun King with fresh fruit every day of the year.

With the excitement of new projects it is easy to neglect one's least favourite parts of the garden. Things change so quickly. One year a feature can look wonderful and by the next it has become overgrown; one needs to keep constant vigilance. One of my great pleasures is walking round with friends whose knowledge and judgement I particularly respect and are generous enough to make suggestions. After all, I know I cannot make anything new, it has all been done before; but I can try to bring together all the best ideas passed on to me by present-day friends and old-fashioned writers and combine them with my own thoughts and so, I hope, create a garden which feels loved and longs to be walked in.

Rosemary Verey

186 The vegetable garden follows an adapted 17th-century design. The paths create narrow beds, which are easy to maintain as well as being decorative

Bramdean House, Alresford, Hampshire

Mrs Hady Wakefield's Garden

Bramdean overlooks an extremely busy main road between Winchester and Petersfield, from which it is protected by a massive box and yew hedge, shaped by the years and clipped into eccentric domed undulations which remind one of recumbent elephants. Behind this bastion and the house one is unaware of the medium-sized chalk garden which slopes gently away to the north. It is divided into three sections: the herbaceous garden with long borders, lawns and terracing; the walled garden which is mostly fruit and vegetables; and beyond that the orchard with the clocktower at the end of the vista.

Though I have lived here most of my life, I must immediately say that my mother created the garden, and I inherited it after her unexpected death in 1975. We are very fortunate in having Mr Sivier, who has been gardener here for eighteen years and provides a valuable and splendid link, helped in the afternoons by Mrs Sivier.

The long herbaceous borders which stretch away from the house are most important features of the garden and need careful thought as they are seen from so many angles. We have to make selective

187 *The orchard at Bramdean House in spring. The central path is bordered with mixed daffodils under flowering cherries and Irish yews.*

188 *Looking across the herbaceous garden towards the first iron gate leading into the walled garden. Clipped box forms a feature behind the borders*

189 (Left) *The vista from the house, between well-established herbaceous borders*

190 (Right) *In the walled garden. The sun dial stands in a circle of lawn surrounded by clipped yews*

divisions each year, trying to balance both shape and colour. There is a predominance of blue in the early summer which is then overtaken by yellow. We were very lucky to lose so little during the drought of 1976, due partly, no doubt, to the plants being long-established and well manured annually.

Many of the older apple trees in the orchard have clematis, honeysuckle or roses climbing through them. Irish yews tied into conical shapes are planted at intervals beside the central grass path, and in spring a multitude of daffodils spreads in large drifts all over the orchard. At the end of the vista is an old apple house, topped by a clocktower; the door is painted bright cornflower blue, a surprisingly successful choice. Some beehives which originally belonged to my grandmother live in the orchard. The bees are of the utmost value for the pollination, though it may not be generally known that they only work single flowers. We produce our own honey, and are entirely self-supporting as far as vegetables and most fruits are concerned.

A large garden is a heavy responsibility yet the pleasure Bramdean gives us, and many others, far outweighs the problems. Certainly it provides constant occupation. We never cease to experiment and learn, and the common bond of gardening is an exceptionally strong one.

Victoria Wakefield

191 and 192 *Looking towards the house along the central grass path in the walled garden. The beds are triangular, half of them filled with massed antirrhinums, and in the reverse triangles are floribunda roses 'Iceberg', 'Firecracker' and 'Dickson's Flame'*

145

Hill House, Wickwar, Gloucestershire

Sally, Duchess of Westminster's Garden

MY FIRST love-affair was with Maggie Mott, a viola. I was about six. My sisters and I had been given a few packets of flower seeds and three narrow strips in a tight border. I was lyrical with anticipation. They were plainly bored and a bit nappy at having to labour with the sets of tools inscribed with our names. Thirty years later I found myself with a garden of my own and a husband who looked on appreciatively but did not participate.

I found this place ten years ago when I had to move from Cheshire, decided it had great potential as a garden and bought it immediately. There were seven and a half acres of very flat land, over half of which were within a walled enclosure. The remaining three acres were paddock and I gave two of them over to a scheme of trees, shrubs and Rugosa roses, all of which look after themselves with a minimum of fuss. I kept the rest for a small flock of black Welsh mountain sheep.

Someone in the past had troubled to make a collection of fine trees. Still standing are beeches, green and copper, cedars, a massive yew, a well-placed *Tilia petiolaris*, some pines, larches and the tallest *Ailanthus altissima* ever, aptly called the 'Tree of Heaven'. The yew makes a backdrop for a wire pleasure dome constructed in the eighteenth-century manner, which is smothered with clematis, a *Lonicera tragophylla* and swags of the prolific white-blossomed rambler Ednaston 'climber', twining unhindered into the bulk of the tree.

I arrived here on the coldest November day possible, towing a horse-box crammed with surplus

193 A spring corner with a dramatic planting of Euphorbia wulfenii *and a variegated yucca*

194 One of the white ramblers effectively planted beside a mixed border in July

195 *A statue by Sean Crampton, where gold interspersed with silver shrubs is the dominant motive*

trees, shrubs and plants from my garden at Saighton in Cheshire which I had started eighteen years before. I had already emptied all the Hill House borders, changed their shapes, double-dug and horse-manured them. Three men and I were obsessed with getting everything in at once, to protect the new arrivals.

I had a pink chestnut, a topless cedar and a tired larch removed from the paddock and this made the garden seem even flatter, not a knoll or slope to break it up. One alternative would have been to go for a formal layout, but that was not in keeping with my character. I far prefer irregular shapes and experimental effects.

I laid down a 'promenade' of mown grass flanked by gold and silver trees and shrubs embedded in golden gravel. This was to give a basic luminous effect. At one end is a statue by Sean Crampton of one of the Three Kings. I have been asked more than once if it is me riding home after a day's hunting. In the other direction you walk towards a lovely silver-margined *Aralia*. There is a curving line of fastigiate yews, a group of pencil-thin Skyrocket and several *Eucalyptus* grown from seed, now twelve to twenty feet high. Mown paths among the rough grass help to make the area more interesting, I hope. To get some height I planted a double row of pleached red-twigged limes, supplied by James Smith of Matlock. I ordered small trees and therefore they were cheap. I was prepared to wait five or six years and now they are quite effective.

Four fifteenth-century Veronese columns divide the mown grass from the rough and are over-shadowed by a huge weeping birch. I was also lucky to inherit a south-west facing wall, one hundred feet long and twelve feet high, against which *Carpenteria californica*, *Feijoa sellowiana*, *Ptelea trifoliata* 'Aurea' and a Banksian rose seem to be happy with a number of *Hebe*, *Coronilla* and *Cistus*. at their feet.

The neutral soil had not been cultivated within living memory, and almost everything I planted shot up with speed. 'Your instant garden', one friend called it, after only three or four years.

Not being remotely methodical, I do not plan on paper and, in consequence, rarely achieve

147

196 A bush of Hebe *'Midsummer Beauty'*
dominates a corner of the huge mixed border

197 A high brick wall running the whole length of the
garden provides shelter

symmetry. I try never to repeat any success I may have stumbled on, over grouping or underplanting. There are a thousand combinations of colour and form to try out. I instinctively plant aromatic shrubs at strategic points where visitors cannot help but brush against them.

Facing the front door is a second paddock which originally had a farm gate. I replaced this with a pair of Lutyens urns and asked an architect friend to rough out a design of circular steps that now lead to a planting of evergreen trees interspersed with *Prunus subhirtella* 'Autumnalis'.

There is a small pond near the house as I like to hear the sound of splashing water from my bed. I had to remove a chimney breast from inside the house and with the immense quantity of stone I made a bank, having first dug out a small area, lined it with polythene and filled it with water from the mains. Willows now give shade and secrecy to the goldfish, and the garden birds use it for drinking.

I have two flights planted up for foreign birds. One in an ancient greenhouse with the glass replaced by wire. Redrumps, cockateel and canaries breed happily, and the quail particularly enjoy the cover from ground elder. Buddleias grown from seed and *Sambucus* have shot through the wire roof, which gives protection from the sun and lofty perching places.

I love working in the garden myself, regardless of whatever help I can get – at the moment I have one O.A.P. I enjoy weeding and scrabbling on all fours under my shrubs doing battle with bindweed and outwitting the ground elder. After a long session I am almost an ambulance case. One day I may find myself marching through the Golden Gates before my time ripped to bits by the thorny arms of 'Cerise Bouquet'. But to me it is worth suffering such indignities when I remember the years I have spent in a kind of delirium, always with an eye to the next season and its unknown delights.

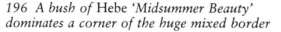

Lyegrove, Badminton, Avon

The Dowager Countess of Westmorland's Garden

WE BOUGHT Lyegrove from the late Duke of Beaufort, in the 1920s. The house was lit by gas, a do-it-yourself affair, not at all satisfactory, giving a dim light and on the smelly side. There was a shortage of bathrooms, an abundance of ugly ceilings and no heating. We had to put in a new staircase and cornices, as well as new plumbing and electricity. Mr Kitchin, an architect who lived at Winchester and was highly recommended, came to our rescue, not only to organize the work indoors, but also to plan the garden which was almost non-existent.

It was, simply, a very large walled kitchen garden. In my dreams, though, I had always wanted high walls for climbing roses and all the other lovely creepers. Mr Kitchin began by making a sunken lily-pool where cabbages and Brussels sprouts had grown. The pool was a pretty shape, surrounded by paving and retaining walls of Cotswold stone, reached on each of the four sides by shallow steps. I decided to leave the old apple trees; they bore no fruit, but the blossom in spring was enchanting. Yew

198 *The terrace on the south side of the house at Lyegrove. By the front door is one of the many magnolias planted by Lady Westmorland in the early twenties, when she started the garden*

199 The Georgian summerhouse and sunken lawn gardens. Over the wall cascades Rosa 'Raubritter'

200 A spectacular border of Pacific hybrid delphiniums edged with nepeta

hedges were planted, making as it were four rooms; and a gateway of Georgian design with a pediment and niches was built on the south side. The other original entrance to the garden was a small wooden gate in the wall, painted green. But on the terrace by a grove of trees, after which Lyegrove was partly named, there happened to be a summer house completely covered with ivy. This turned out to be early Georgian with stone arches and balustrading, and had a pair of superb eighteenth-century stone gate-piers with shell-headed niches on both sides. I had these pillars moved stone by stone and re-erected where the green door had been. They made a fine entrance to the garden. More shallow steps led from there to the lily-pool.

Planting the ornamental cherries, the magnolias and bush-roses, and generally thinking things out, took me at least seven years. It was my first effort. In those days there was no National Gardens

201 Part of the walled garden, where rambling and climbing roses flourish

202 Massed annuals, with regale lilies and delphiniums in the picking border

203 *The sunken lily pool, which is surrounded by mellowed Cotswold stone*
paving, interspersed with valerian, irises, pinks, helianthemums, campanulas and
many other plants. The elegant 18th-century stone gate-piers can be seen in the background

Scheme; as a rule gardens were not open to the public, and people were not so interested in gardening. I had little knowledge of plants, what they should be and where they should be planted, and equally knew little about soil and aspects. The soil at Lyegrove is limey, and I remember buying camellias, *auratum* lilies and lots of peat-loving things. After a year the lime had got through, so that was the end of them. I made many other mistakes; plants constantly had to be dug up and replanted elsewhere.

After approximately six years I had got the garden more or less established. Plants were beginning to do well and I was fairly satisfied. But I had a great longing to enlarge the garden and became increasingly restless. I needed more scope and more room to plant all the lovely shrubs I had seen in other people's gardens, gardens famous for their beauty such as Hidcote, Sissinghurst, Norah Lindsay's at Sutton Courtenay and Miss Jekyll's at Munstead Wood. I decided to take in the field beyond the garden wall.

It was a big undertaking, and I had no Mr Kitchin to advise me, and apart from my gardeners and myself, only a local builder and many willing hands to dig and carry earth.

The first thing I did was to move the Georgian summer house, again stone by stone, from the terrace to a site some hundred yards away. The cost was £78; I tremble to think what it would be nowadays. The garden was surrounded with yew hedges for shelter and I planted an avenue of ornamental double white cherry trees called *Prunus cerasus* 'Rhexii', which led the eye to the summer house at the far end of the new garden. On each side of the avenue I dug out sunken lawn-gardens with low retaining walls. Rambler and climbing roses were intended to tumble over these walls. The soil from the sunken gardens made a raised herbaceous border, where I planted Pacific hybrid delphiniums, campanulas, eremurus, paeonies and many other flowers. How extraordinary to think that this planting was done about fifty years ago and the general effect is still the same.

I have always liked this garden best, particularly in spring, perhaps because the spring gives me a special joy of anticipation and excitement. The magnolias are in flower, the roses full of bud, the cherries blossoming, the different coloured *Aubrietas,* the rock roses and foxgloves – indeed too many names to recall – are either out or coming on.

Together, my summer garden and my spring garden measure one and a half acres. I also have lawns round the house, a mown terrace and a grove with its colony of rooks. The grove is raised above the level of the lawns, while under the trees are expanses of rough grass, white with snowdrops in early spring. Daffodils, which are always multiplying and spreading, cherries and other shrubs flourish here as well. In the summer it is a great delight walking through cow-parsley shoulder high.

I think levels and vistas are very important when planning a garden, and above all good well-mown lawns and not too many borders. In borders I like big groups, not just one or two of a single specimen, which is inclined to look spotty. Then there are the weeds, usually banished by gardeners. I have a large group of magnolias with a carpet of the little blue *Veronica* called speedwell; I love the effect. I also love the wild geraniums and meadowsweet. I treasure all flowers. My garden has a formal layout, but I have tried to make the overall effect as informal as possible. In my view bush roses should be allowed to ramp but climbing roses should be ruthlessly pruned and never allowed to get to the top of walls, leaving naked stems below.

The design of my garden was complete in about 1935, but it has, of course, needed and taken many years to mature and to weather the setbacks I have had. Even now there is still so much to be done and so little time.

Diana Westmorland

Index

Page numbers in *italics* refer to illustrations

153